MW00804565

10 Church Street
Silver Springs, NY 14550

BUYING/SELLING YOUR HOME MADE E-Z

FE '00

TOWN OF GAINESVILLE
PUBLIC LIBRARY
10 Church Street
Silver Springs, NY 14550

MADE E-Z PRODUCTS, Inc.
Deerfield Beach, Florida / www.MadeE-Z.com

NOTICE:

THIS PRODUCT IS NOT INTENDED TO PROVIDE LEGAL ADVICE. IT CONTAINS GENERAL INFORMATION FOR EDUCATIONAL PURPOSES ONLY. PLEASE CONSULT AN ATTORNEY IN ALL LEGAL MATTERS. THIS PRODUCT WAS NOT PREPARED BY A PERSON LICENSED TO PRACTICE LAW IN THIS STATE.

Buying/Selling Your Home Made E-Z™
Copyright 2000 Made E-Z Products, Inc.
Printed in the United States of America

MADE E-Z
PRODUCTS

384 South Military Trail
Deerfield Beach, FL 33442
Tel. 954-480-8933
Fax 954-480-8906

http://www.MadeE-Z.com
All rights reserved.

1 2 3 4 5 6 7 8 9 10   CPC   R   10 9 8 7 6 5 4 3 2

This publication is designed to provide accurate and authoritative information in regard to subject matter covered. It is sold with the understanding that neither the publisher nor author is engaged in rendering legal, accounting, or other professional services. If legal advice or other expert assistance is required, the services of a competent professional should be sought. From: *A Declaration of Principles jointly adopted by a Committee of the American Bar Association and a Committee of Publishers.*

Buying/Selling Your Home Made E-Z™

Important Notice

This product is intended for informational use only and is not a substitute for legal advice. State laws vary and change and the information or forms do not necessarily conform to the laws or requirements of your state. While you always have the right to prepare your own documents and to act as your own attorney, do consult an attorney on all important legal matters. You will find a listing of state bar referral services in the Resources section of this product. This product was not prepared by a person licensed to practice law in this state.

Limited warranty and disclaimer

This self-help product is intended to be used by the consumer for his/her own benefit. It may not be reproduced in whole or in part, resold or used for commercial purposes without written permission from the publisher. In addition to copyright violations, the unauthorized reproduction and use of this product to benefit a second party may be considered the unauthorized practice of law.

This product is designed to provide authoritative and accurate information in regard to the subject matter covered. However, the accuracy of the information is not guaranteed, as laws and regulations may change or be subject to differing interpretations. Consequently, you may be responsible for following alternative procedures, or using material or forms different from those supplied with this product. It is strongly advised that you examine the laws of your state before acting upon any of the material contained in this product.

As with any matter, common sense should determine whether you need the assistance of an attorney. We urge you to consult with an attorney, qualified estate planner, or tax professional, or to seek any other relevant expert advice whenever substantial sums of money are involved, you doubt the suitability of the product you have purchased, or if there is anything about the product that you do not understand including its adequacy to protect you. Even if you are completely satisfied with this product, we encourage you to have your attorney review it.

Neither the author, publisher, distributor nor retailer are engaged in rendering legal, accounting or other professional services. Accordingly, the publisher, author, distributor and retailer shall have neither liability nor responsibility to any party for any loss or damage caused or alleged to be caused by the use of this product.

Copyright Notice

The purchaser of this guide is hereby authorized to reproduce in any form or by any means, electronic or mechanical, including photocopying, all forms and documents contained in this guide, provided it is for non-profit, educational or private use. Such reproduction requires no further permission from the publisher and/or payment of any permission fee.

The reproduction of any form or document in any other publication intended for sale is prohibited without the written permission of the publisher. Publication for nonprofit use should provide proper attribution to Made E-Z Products.

Table of contents

How to use this guide

The Made E-Z™ guides can help you achieve an important legal objective conveniently, efficiently and economically. But it is important to properly use this guide if you are to avoid later difficulties.

◆ Carefully read all information, warnings and disclaimers concerning the legal forms in this guide. If after thorough examination you decide that you have circumstances that are not covered by the forms in this guide, or you do not feel confident about preparing your own documents, consult an attorney.

◆ Complete each blank on each legal form. Do not skip over inapplicable blanks or lines intended to be completed. If the blank is inapplicable, mark "N/A" or "None" or use a dash. This shows you have not overlooked the item.

◆ Always use pen or type on legal documents—never use pencil.

◆ Avoid erasures and "cross-outs" on final documents. Use photocopies of each document as worksheets, or as final copies. All documents submitted to the court must be printed on one side only.

◆ Correspondence forms may be reproduced on your own letterhead if you prefer.

◆ Whenever legal documents are to be executed by a partnership or corporation, the signatory should designate his or her title.

◆ It is important to remember that on legal contracts or agreements between parties all terms and conditions must be clearly stated. Provisions may not be enforceable unless in writing. All parties to the agreement should receive a copy.

◆ Instructions contained in this guide are for your benefit and protection, so follow them closely.

◆ You will find a glossary of useful terms at the end of this guide. Refer to this glossary if you encounter unfamiliar terms.

◆ Always keep legal documents in a safe place and in a location known to your spouse, family, personal representative or attorney.

Introduction to Buying/ Selling Your Home Made E-Z™

Buying or selling a home is often the largest single transaction you make during your lifetime. If you are buying, you will likely spend much of the rest of your life paying off your home through some type of mortgage. The last thing you need to do is pay more than you can afford, or more than a house is worth. Prequalifying for a mortgage before you look at particular homes gives you focus, and consulting an appraiser can provide an honest perspective on a home's value.

If you are selling, you may have the opportunity to realize large profits, or at least cut serious losses. Be adequately prepared to seize these opportunities by properly pricing, advertising and showing your home.

Hiring a real estate agent usually will cost you an additional six percent in commission. Often real estate agents know little more about a property's value than you. A real estate agent's ultimate goal is to make a sale and generate commission—period. The particular house you find as a buyer, or the price you settle on as a seller, is secondary. Keep this in mind before you commit, and understand the responsibilities you would take on if you decide to "go it alone."

A home is usually much more than just a financial investment— "home is where the heart is." You and your family will likely spend endless hours sleeping, eating and entertaining there. Making the right decisions before you buy or sell can help save you money or realize profit, but it can also make the difference between years of comfort and countless sleepless nights wondering where you went wrong. As a buyer, this involves prioritizing your needs and desires, thoroughly inspecting the homes you are interested in and selecting the home that is right for you.

As anyone who has bought or sold a home will attest, timing can be critical and the process quite stressful. Many sellers are also in the process of buying another home, and if they sell their home quickly they may not be able to afford to board in a hotel or stay with relatives for months while waiting to close on a new home. Likewise, many sellers will have their homes on the market for a year or more without finding a buyer. After some time, they may be forced to settle for a much lower price, especially if the buyer senses an extreme urgency to sell. In both buying and selling, desperation is costly, but it can be avoided by being prepared.

You might find the right house at the right price at the right time, and still not be in the clear. Buying or selling a home involves an intricate web of legal issues, from mortgage applications and real estate contracts to title clearances and settlement statements. This guide contains a wealth of information to help you understand basic legal issues you may confront when buying or selling a home. It also contains basic forms you may encounter.

In this guide, you will learn to judge your needs and what you can afford, whether to use a real estate agent, how to evaluate and finance a home, and how to close the sale. This knowledge will save you time and money and keep anxiety to a minimum when buying or selling your home—made E-Z!

Deciding when the time is right

1

Chapter 1

Deciding when the time is right

What you'll find in this chapter:

- ⇒ When you're ready to own
- ⇒ Determining priorities and needs
- ⇒ Knowing when to buy
- ⇒ Alternatives to buying and selling
- ⇒ Costs to consider when buying or selling

Are you ready to become a home owner?

First, consider your own personal circumstances. Maybe you need extra space or privacy because of a recent marriage or an impending birth. You may feel it is time to relocate closer to work, to a better neighborhood, or to a new town altogether. If you are an apartment dweller, you may be tired of paying rent into a bottomless pit.

Second, understand the commitment and responsibility. Granted, your first home probably won't be your last; studies show Americans move every four years. Still, moving is no longer as simple as signing another lease. It is a stressful, time-consuming and expensive process that involves serious investigation. Changes such as a new school, park or commercial development, and even the crime element impact your investment.

Third, decide if it is a good idea financially. You need cash for a down payment and closing costs of at least five percent of a home's price. In addition, you will probably pay higher mortgage payments than you would for rent. You must be able to prove to a lender you have a stable job and credit history. Also, you must be prepared to adopt a rigorous savings plan for meeting all payment schedules including down payment and closing costs, monthly mortgage payments, property taxes, insurance and utilities.

> **note** You buy not only your own property, but also an interest in the community.

Fourth, keep this in mind: buying a home is a long-term investment. Rents may rise, but conventional mortgage payments remain the same even as property values appreciate. Translation: Owning puts you on the profit side of the ledger.

Finally, consider the powerful tax advantages of home ownership. The You may also tap your home equity to obtain interest-deductible loans for improving your home, sending your children to college, retiring or buying another home.

> **STRATEGY** IRS allows homeowners to deduct all mortgage interest, reducing your annual tax bill significantly. This is particularly evident early in the mortgage when a large percentage of each payment pays off the interest.

If you are presently a homeowner, you may be ready to sell in order to repay debt, realize profit, get rid of depreciating property, or upgrade (or downgrade) your living quarters.

Sales Cycles

While all real estate markets vary, each is subject to certain sales cycles which influence market activity and pricing.

Taxes

Some buyers will wait for a hefty IRS return, which usually arrives in early summer, to use as a down payment on a house. Others strive for a January closing in order to get a full 12 months of interest payment deductions to offset a large amount of taxable income.

Weather

In fall and winter, home prices tend to be lower in most parts of the country because of uncertain weather and travel conditions. This especially affects vacant homes. Showing a cold home can turn buyers off and drive down the price. As a buyer, you might profit from finding a home you like during this off-season when fewer shoppers are in the market. However, at the same time fewer sellers will likely put their homes on the market, which can benefit a seller who sells during the off-season.

> HINT Many families with school-age children plan their home purchase around the academic year, since buying during late spring allows them to move into their new home during the summer while school is not in session.

In spring and summer, home prices tend to rise in most parts of the country because sellers anticipate at least six months of good weather—and more daylight hours—to shop for a home, move in and make improvements. In warm weather regions, seasonal trends reverse; the market is more active during fall and winter and drops off during spring and summer.

Holidays

The weeks surrounding Thanksgiving and Christmas and national holidays are not good times to put your home on the market. Many people travel or entertain during these times, thus reducing the pool of potential buyers.

Buyer's or seller's market

DEFINITION

Determining whether it is a buyer's or seller's market requires extensive research and analysis. In a *buyer's market*, more houses are for sale than there are buyers on the market. You can likely pick and choose among a number of homes, take your time, and negotiate your price. In a *seller's market*, more buyers are on the market than houses being sold. Sellers can command their price, and buyers have to act quickly to finalize a sale.

Having enough time

If your documentation is not properly prepared, however, the process can take as long as a year. In most circumstances, time is of the essence; the quicker and more efficiently you get things done, the better.

When buying you should allow yourself at least to six months in order to secure a mortgage and close on a home.

If you are moving out of an apartment, sometimes you can arrange a month-to-month lease. However, if you are selling one house and buying another one, coordinating both transactions at once and moving from one to the other can be a nearly impossible task, not to mention an expensive one. Moving and storing furniture can be costly, and you may have to rent a hotel room, put your belongings into storage, and buy a cellular phone so you can stay in touch with your contacts.

Alternatives to buying and selling

Sometimes you are simply better off not moving. Though you will rarely hear this advice from a real estate agent, you may hear it from someone who has had a bad experience moving, or from someone who has successfully stayed put. The cost of the broker's commission, moving, decorating and closing—combined with the time and stress involved—could make you reconsider. You could expose yourself to possible disaster, such as an unliveable neighborhood, serious problems with the home, debt, or just plain homesickness. Change is not always for the better.

If your problem is not having enough space in your current home, consider remodeling or adding on. Do you like your neighborhood enough to stay? Is ample space available, and do neighborhood codes permit additions? Will the improvements boost the value of your home when you eventually sell? If the answers are "yes," financing is available. Home improvement loans are offered by the Federal Housing Administration and

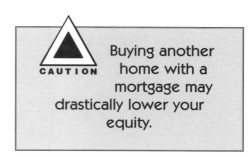

CAUTION Buying another home with a mortgage may drastically lower your equity.

the Federal National Mortgage Association (Fannie Mae) Homestyle Program. Improving your home will build your *home equity*—credit measured by the difference between your home's market value and what you owe on your mortgage.

DEFINITION

If you think you should sell simply to pay off your debts, you should first consider refinancing, securing a second mortgage or tapping your home equity for credit. When making the decision about whether or not to move, consult a number of sources, including not only professionals, such as an accountant, lawyer or lender, but also friends, co-workers, neighbors and relatives.

Determining how much you can afford

2

Chapter 2

Determining how much you can afford

> ### What you'll find in this chapter:
>
> ➠ Qualifying for the loan you want
>
> ➠ Determining your monthly payments
>
> ➠ Can you afford the down payment?
>
> ➠ Cleaning up your credit before you buy
>
> ➠ Prequalifying vs. preapproval

Though you may be tempted, hold off on touring homes until you establish a target price. This saves time and safeguards against disappointment caused by your unrealistic expectations.

How large a loan do you qualify for?

An oversimplified rule says you can qualify for a mortgage of twice your annual household income. This means that if you and your spouse earn $50,000 a year combined, you would qualify for a $100,000 mortgage.

DEFINITION

Along with total household income, lenders are also interested in an applicant's *net worth*, or total assets minus total liabilities. A high net worth will qualify you for a larger loan, a lower down payment and lower interest rates. Each lender has its own form for calculating net worth, you can get started by filling out a Personal Financial Worksheet (see Appendix).

How much will your monthly payments be?

If you are a first-time buyer, you will probably pay a slightly higher monthly mortgage bill than you currently pay in rent. Lenders use mortgage ratios such as 25/33 or 28/36, to determine your monthly payments. The first number is a percentage of gross monthly income; the second is a percentage of gross income minus long-term debts. For example, you gross $2,000 a month and have $400 in long-term debt. Using the 25/33 ratio, you would multiply $2,000 by 0.25 to get $500. Then multiply $1,600 by 0.33 to get $528. The lender would choose the lower total, or $500.

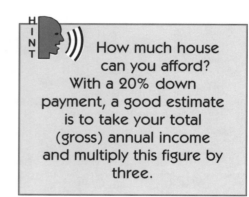

How much house can you afford? With a 20% down payment, a good estimate is to take your total (gross) annual income and multiply this figure by three.

Another way to determine the monthly mortgage payments you can afford is by completing the Monthly Budget Planner (see Appendix). In order to afford your new home, you may need to adjust your lifestyle, focusing on staying home and cutting expenses. Plan to eat out less, watch movies at home instead of in the theater, take fewer vacations and make fewer credit card purchases.

How much cash do you need?

Mortgage lenders generally require a five to 20 percent down payment. Rates tend to be higher in areas where property values are receding and lower where they are appreciating. Lenders make you pay for private mortgage insurance (PMI), which protects them against your default in payments, if your down payment is less than 20 percent. You are allowed to cancel PMI when your equity reaches 20 percent of the value of the home.

Definition:

Closing costs include fees for surveying, appraising, escrowing, researching, copying, attorneys, broker commission, etc.

You may be tempted to use all your savings, even if it exceeds the minimum required by your lender, as a down payment. A large down payment means you need to borrow less, lowering the interest you pay throughout the life of your mortgage. But it also decreases the amount of interest you may deduct from your taxes. It leaves you with less cash for immediate needs such as furnishings, repairs, settlement and moving costs, not to mention future needs such as emergencies, your children's education and retirement.

DEFINITION

Lenders charge *points*, as a percentage of the total loan, for the right to borrow money. A point roughly equals one-eighth of one percentage point on the interest of a 30-year fixed-rate mortgage. You will also pay an origination fee, usually one percent of the loan, when you apply for the loan. It is usually discounted from the total points you will pay at settlement. In addition, you will need to establish an escrow account holding up to 14 months of prepaid taxes, utilities and insurance, until you own 20 percent equity in your home.

You also need cash for closing costs, which typically account for two to four percent of the loan excluding points.

Clean up your credit

Before you apply for a loan, it is imperative that you solidify your credit. Pay off as many consumer loans as possible, including auto loans and outstanding credit card balances. Close all unnecessary credit card accounts, and send a letter to each company asking them to note "closed at request of cardholder" next to the account on your credit report.

 If you are planning to use a gift from relatives as part of your down payment, deposit into your bank account at least six months in advance of your mortgage application; lenders usually ask for bank statements covering the last six months.

Obtain a copy of your credit report from major credit reporting agencies to make certain it contains no surprises. These companies process millions of accounts a year, and mistakes are common. Getting mistakes removed is not difficult, but they will remain until you take action. A good place to begin is with the E-Z Legal Guide to Credit Repair. Your credit report may contain information about your employment history, credit cards, bank accounts, debts and payment history. It may even include information of public record, such as lawsuits and judgments, bankruptcy, divorce, foreclosure, tax liens, wage garnishment and even criminal convictions. Take care of any unpaid collections, such as bounced check charges or back taxes, and have references to them removed.

If you cannot get certain marks removed, you can at least attach a "consumer statement" explaining the specifics in your report. For instance, you could show that during a period of unemployment you worked as an independent contractor, or that a bankruptcy was caused by the death of a business partner.

Prequalification vs. preapproval

DEFINITION *Prequalifying* is an unofficial, initial estimate of the size mortgage you can afford. It may be done over the telephone or online, without supplying any documentation. *Preapproval* is an underwriter's documented guarantee of a specific loan amount. It certifies that the lender has reviewed all your paperwork, including tax returns, check stubs, net worth statements, monthly budget worksheets, and so on. Having this certified proof of financial readiness gives you bargaining power when you find a home you like. It also helps speed up the loan application process after you have made an offer.

Using an agent or doing it yourself

3

Chapter 3

Using an agent or doing it yourself

What you'll find in this chapter:

➠ Should you use a real estate agent?

➠ How to select a real estate agent

➠ Why you need a listing agreement

➠ How to "do it yourself"

➠ The ins and outs of real estate classified ads

Once you have an idea of what type of home you are after, you need to decide whether to proceed with some type of agent or on your own. agents typically charge about six percent commission on a sale. For a $100,000 house, that is $6,000!

Many real estate representatives prove to be excellent resources for finding you a home or a buyer, judging the market, and taking care of all the complicated and time-consuming work. They have access to Multiple Listing Services, the most complete computer database of homes on the market, and are trained to find the one that's right for each individual buyer.

Others have little expertise but are punchy sales personalities out to make big bucks without exerting much effort. They take short courses for certification, lack experience, receive no formal training in home appraisal, and concentrate on making a quick sale rather than meeting the buyer's needs.

Are the services they provide worth that much, or is it worth it to do it yourself and save the fee? If you decide to hire a representative, make sure you are comfortable with him or her and with the agreement you have signed.

Choosing the right agent

The right agent is the one who helps find the right home for the buyer or the right buyer for the seller. The two most common ways to find an agent are:

- Word of mouth: Friends or relatives with values similar to your own may have had success with a particular agent and would enthusiastically recommend that agent to you. This referral can be a valuable source of information. They may also tell you whom to avoid.

> *note*
> A Realtor® is a member of the National Association of Realtors. A Realtor Associate works for a Realtor. A broker is licensed by the state. An agent is usually an independent contractor working for a broker.

- By location: Often agents specialize in particular areas, developments, types of homes, builders, or just about any other method by which homes can be classified. These agents often advertise their specialties in newspapers and local real estate publications.

Types of real estate agents

Regardless of how you select a agent, it is important to know the different types of agents and whom they work for. Do not assume any agent you do business with is working for you. Most agents work with buyers, but they also work for sellers.

DEFINITION

This kind of agent is known as a *seller's broker*. This is, for example, the agent whose name appears on the "for sale" sign in the front yard. This agent has a sole and exclusive contractual responsibility to the seller, a responsibility to get the highest possible price for the home in the shortest time. The seller's agent receives a commission for the sale from the seller. You may deliver an offer to this agent and he or she is obligated to deliver it to the seller. Once an offer is accepted by the seller, it is this agent's job to keep the buyer from changing his or her mind and, thus, to close the sale.

DEFINITION

The *buyer's broker* works exclusively for the buyer. The buyer, not the seller, pays the commission. Since sellers usually pay commissions out of the proceeds of the sale and this fee is built into the price of the home, it is said the buyer always pays the commission. However, if you as the buyer also have to pay your buyer's agent, you have an additional expense. Nevertheless, this kind of agent is increasingly popular. Because this agent's commission comes exclusively from the buyer, it is believed he or she will follow the buyer's best interests. Check your state's laws governing agency for the definition and legality of a buyer's agent.

DEFINITION

A *buyer's Realtor* is the traditional real estate agent who first works for the buyer by helping to find him or her a home. But once the home is found and an offer is made, this agent's goal is to close the deal, since he or she gets paid commission by the seller. This is the most common arrangement.

Interviewing the agent

To find the right agent, you must begin with an interview, as you would with any new employee. You should ask the following questions of any potential agent:

1) *How long have you been with your current firm?* If the agent has been with the firm for less than a year, ask how long he or she has been an agent. If this is not his or her first job as a agent, find out where the agent has worked before. If the person had unrelated

realty experience, such as commercial or corporate realty, ask about his or her motives for switching to residential.

2) *Can you provide past and current references?* While most agents will readily supply references from past clients, you should also request references from current clients. Follow up on these references to get a feeling for how the agent's current relationships are doing. Ask:

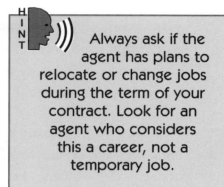

Always ask if the agent has plans to relocate or change jobs during the term of your contract. Look for an agent who considers this a career, not a temporary job.

- How long was the house on the market?

- How close to the original price did it sell for?

- How many times did you renew the listing with the same agent?

- Did you accept the offer based on what you thought was a good deal, or because of outside pressures?

- Did other agents in the office show your home to buyers?

A real estate firm might offer additional resources, but find out if the firm is receiving a "kickback" for delivering these services.

- Did the agent appear at the closing?

- Was the firm generally pleasant to do business with?

- Would you use the same agent again?

3) *What additional services can your firm provide?* Does the firm work with specific mortgage lenders, inspectors, title companies, repairmen or insurance companies? The more resources you can draw on, the more value you receive for your time and commission payout. Even so, you must balance the value of your time against paying a higher fee.

4) *What kind of game plan can you outline?* Knowing what to expect from your agent and when to expect it helps reduce some of the mystery and anxiety associated with buying or selling a home. Ask yourself the following:

- Does the agent's plan seem realistic and logical?

- Does it seem well thought out based upon years of experience or is it improvised on the spot?

- Is the agent willing to justify a particular step?

- What if it just isn't working? Does the agent have an alternative plan(s)?

- Is he or she willing to customize the plan to suit your particular needs?

- Does the plan include advertising? If so, where?

- What type of market is the agent seeking?

- Is your agent willing to schedule appointments for viewing homes?

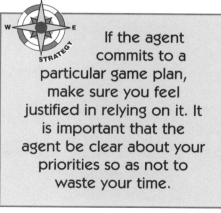

If the agent commits to a particular game plan, make sure you feel justified in relying on it. It is important that the agent be clear about your priorities so as not to waste your time.

5) *Will you screen the homes or buyers in my price range?* You don't want a agent to waste your time with properties or buyers of marginal qualification or interest. You want a agent who will sell your home or find you one within your budget.

You will want additional answers to the following questions from any potential agent:

- How many exclusive listings in your area has he or she had?

- How many closings in the last six months?

- What is the average time from listing to closing?

- Does the agent use a Multiple Listing Service or a nationwide referral service?

- How much advertising does the firm do?

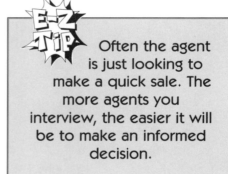

Often the agent is just looking to make a quick sale. The more agents you interview, the easier it will be to make an informed decision.

- How large is his or her staff?

- Is the staff full-time or part-time?

- Does the agent hold open house?

- Does the agent help arrange financing for buyers?

As a seller, do not select a agent just because he or she suggested the highest selling price. This price may be unrealistic and simply be the "bait" before the "switch" to a lower price. You also must be wary of prices that are too low. Prices that cluster around a central figure tend to be the most realistic. Throw out the highest and lowest prices.

Ask for a market analysis for your area. This should include:

- the price that homes comparable to yours have sold for or are currently selling for

- the length of time they have been on the market

- a description of the property

- any dates of sale

After analyzing this list, establish a price with your agent based in part on how quickly you need to sell your home.

When hiring a agent to work with you, expect to sign a written agreement. This is, in effect, an employment contract, and the agreement may be informal or complex.

This agreement should outline the duties and responsibilities that you and your agent have to each other. It is a good idea to insert a clause in the contract allowing you to cancel within the first 48 hours if you are not satisfied with the agent. You will, however, be responsible for the commission on any transactions, if viewed within that 48-hour period. This period of responsibility will be spelled out in the terms of your contract.

CAUTION Be sure to read any written agreement with your agent carefully, and have anything you do not understand explained in clear language.

Types of listing agreements

If you are selling a home, you will be asked to sign a listing agreement. This listing outlines the terms and conditions of the sale, including whether the agent has an exclusive right, for a specified time, to market the home.

There are three types of listing agreements:

1) **Exclusive right to sell.** The agent who takes the listing receives a commission regardless of who actually sells the home, even if you sell the home yourself. If another agent sells the home, the commission is divided between the agents.

2) **Exclusive agency.** You pay no commission to the agent if you sell the home yourself. This is usually used when you find someone who is interested in purchasing your home prior to hiring a agent and is often limited to that particular party.

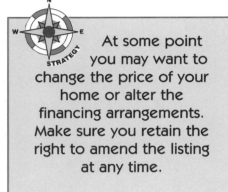

At some point you may want to change the price of your home or alter the financing arrangements. Make sure you retain the right to amend the listing at any time.

3) **Open listing.** You pay a commission if, and only if, the agent finds a buyer before you do. Since you are willing to work at least as hard as your agent to find a buyer, agents often accept about half the regular commission rate on this type of sale. Remember if you have an open listing with one agent, you cannot sign an exclusive agreement with another until your open listing has expired.

If the agent presents you with a buyer who is prepared to purchase your home and meets the terms and conditions of the listing, you are obligated to pay the agent's commission. You must do this even if you reject the deal!

Do some of the legwork

You may be able to negotiate lower commission by agreeing to handle some of the tasks yourself, limiting the services and time required of your agent. Make your own appointments from lists the agent provides, do your own chauffeuring, write your own offer, negotiate your own mortgage, or arrange for your own inspections. Beware of agents who are paid a special bonus by the seller. It may mean the selling price is well above the home's actual value.

Proceeding without an agent

About one in four homes in the U.S. is bought or sold "by owner." First-time buyers must beware of the usual pitfalls such as improper planning, insufficient time and lack of patience. But you can do it if you are market wise and adequately prepared. Before you "do it yourself," learn as much as you can about the responsibilities you will be facing.

Advantages

The main advantage is saving the cost of commission paid to a agent. You also:

- maintain greater control and maximum flexibility over all aspects of the transaction

- decide how and when to advertise

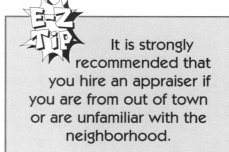

It is strongly recommended that you hire an appraiser if you are from out of town or are unfamiliar with the neighborhood.

- decide what homes to see and when to see them

- decide how to price your home

- control when and to whom you show your home

- can remain on the premises to answer questions when buyers come to inspect it

- get immediate feedback from potential buyers and sellers

- are under no obligation to accept any offer

- do not have to keep a "lock box" on your door

Disadvantages

"Doing it yourself" can be frustrating, time-consuming and expensive. You:

- may waste time and energy seeing unqualified buyers or viewing unwanted homes

- will not get to see homes in a market that are only shown to those buyers who sign an exclusive agreement with a agent

- will have little or no access to data about past sales, current market values and conditions, multiple listing service and agent contacts

- are responsible for deciding if your initial strategy is working and for preparing alternative plans if it isn't

- have to negotiate directly with concerned parties

- will need extreme patience in dealing directly with the public on a regular basis

- will need to pay for advertising, fact sheets and open house signs, in advance

If you are not going to use a agent, hire an attorney for the closing because every state has different laws governing real estate sales and the transfer of property.

- cannot show your home when you are not there

- put undue wear and tear on your vehicle

- must seek out and investigate qualified inspectors, repairmen, lenders, surveyors, insurance companies, appraisers, title companies and attorneys

The classified ad

A key element in successfully selling your own home is placing the proper ad. If you are searching for a home to buy, you must also know how to read and interpret a real estate ad. Real estate ads generally appear in the classified section of the local newspaper. Larger newspapers often have a special weekly real estate section devoted to these ads. Also, find out if any independent realty flyers are published for your area. These have smaller circulation but are exclusively targeted to home buyers, often include small photos, and can be quite effective marketing tools.

> Your classified ad should promote your home's features and its value, attract interest from qualified buyers and motivate them to take a serious look.

 Be sure the advertising medium you choose is appropriate for your target audience. A $30,000 home may sell in a "Bargain Shopper" weekly. A $3,000,000 home would have no business in a "Bargain Shopper," or probably even the local paper, but would be better suited for a prestigious full-color statewide or regional publication.

Each word in an ad is pivotal toward describing and selling your home. Do not rely upon the classified department to write the ad for you. Have it clearly written and tested before you call the newspaper. Show it to friends or relatives and ask if they would respond to it if they were looking for a home.

What to include in your ad

Your ad should convey the following information:

- there is no commission because you are selling the home yourself

- the home is an outstanding buy relative to similar homes on the market

- the home is open to inspection to all interested parties

- location of the home

- asking price of the home

- phone number to call for more information

- a description of the home:

    a) style of home (ex. ranch, split level, colonial)

    b) number of bedrooms

    c) number of bathrooms

    d) special rooms, such as garage, den, workshop or family room

    e) special features, such as fireplace, pool, barbecue pit, tennis court, Jacuzzi, tiled floors, ceiling fans, bay windows, landscaping, patio, lake, etc.

Sample classified ad for real estate:

> **SOUTH ANYCITY – BY OWNER**
> 4 BR ranch w/pool tennis lake patio
> DinRm FmlyRm LivRm 3 1/2 baths
> $175,000 or best reasonable offer
> Inspection daily 5-8 pm Sat.-Sun. 9-6
> Motivated seller (123) 456-7890

Basic format for the ad:

- line 1 in the sample above tells the general location and the fact that there are no commissions involved

- lines 2 and 3 describe the home and highlight its features

- line 4 suggests a negotiable starting price (If the price is not negotiable, include the word "firm.")

- line 5 explains when the home is open for inspection

- line 6 underscores that the price is negotiable and provides the telephone number to call for more information

Depending upon the description of your home, you may add or delete an item, but always include the price.

If you have written and placed a proper ad, you should receive responses the day it appears or by the next day, at the latest. If you are disappointed in the number of responses, first make sure the ad ran as you placed it, and then consider altering the ad. The problem is usually the price. Even listing an undesirable address usually will attract speculators and gamblers.

 For the independent buyer, classifieds can be the gateway to information. As morbid as it may sound, some buyers bargain hunt by turning to the obituary section to find out names and addresses of the deceased. After a reasonable time, they contact relatives and respectfully inquire about the sale of the vacated property.

Open house

Sellers who do without an agent will likely conduct an open house. A bright, attractive yard sign should include your telephone number and a convenient time to call. If potential visitors want directions, mailing or faxing them a clear map outlining the best route helps assure they won't get lost.

 Make up a facts sheet describing your house and its amenities. Most visitors are reluctant to take notes on their own, but will likely hang onto information you provide.

Once they arrive, give them a friendly greeting and a facts sheet. Ask them to sign a ledger and to provide a telephone number. Secure all small, valuable objects. Be friendly and informative, but also unobtrusive. Some visitors want to observe and comment privately. Others may want to negotiate right away. Avoid negotiating the price orally, but be prepared to have the prospective buyer complete a county-approved buyer qualification form. Ask your local county real estate board or county Board of Realtors for these forms.

If you are an independent buyer visiting an open house, be aware that most are conducted by the seller's agent. You may remain anonymous or explain that you are working as your own agent. This will help avoid misunderstandings over commission. Be selective among houses you are viewing to avoid burnout and limit your search to properties you can afford. An agent who shows you a house for the first time usually receives some commission. If you close the deal with another agent, you may have to share commission with the first agent. Avoid needless distractions; leave your kids and pet at home.

Considering different types of homes

Chapter 4

Considering different types of homes

What you'll find in this chapter:

- What home type is best for your family?
- Advantages of the single-family home
- Hidden costs of the "fixer-upper"
- When you own multi-family property
- Condos, foreclosures, and mobile homes

What type of home is right for you? When one envisions owning "The American Dream," a single-family home usually comes to mind. But keep in mind other options, such as a townhome, condominium and mobile home.

Single-family homes

Single-family homes offer an array of benefits, along with several drawbacks. A single-family home typically provides more space, privacy and freedom than a multiple-family dwelling. The emotional attachment grows much deeper; a single-family home evokes a sense of pride, security, and freedom of expression. Many owners spend entire weekends mowing the lawn, manicuring shrubbery, painting window frames, adding new furnishings, and making their home a more personalized part of their lives.

Owning a single-family home also comes with major responsibilities. You pay for utilities, garbage removal, pesticides and just about anything else that may need care or repair. Maintenance costs typically add up to at least three percent of the home's total value. You are also head of security for your home. This may mean buying an alarm system or using a watchdog. Just like a used automobile, a previously owned home comes with its own share of defects, from a leaky faucet to a leaky roof—or much worse.

Building a new home

If you have the money, perhaps the best way to meet all your needs right away is to have a new home built for you. Because appliances and utilities will be modern and efficient, you should not expect significant repair or renovation costs for some time. But you do pay the price for perfection. From the purchase of property and materials to architectural work and detailed labor, it usually adds up to much more than the cost of a previously owned structure. You will essentially be selecting and paying for each itemized feature brand new. Property taxes tend to be high, as areas under construction still need to pay for roads, sidewalks, lighting, civic improvements, etc. Many construction companies don't do landscaping, so you may need to contract with a landscaping company separately to make sure your beautiful new home is not sitting in an unsightly barren lot.

> **HINT**
> Although pre-construction prices are usually lower, sometimes you can save thousands by buying after construction is underway, especially if the buyer has backed out or defaulted, or the builder is using the home for speculation.

The first rule in buying a new home is to select a reputable builder. You can usually get information from the Better Business Bureau or a local builder's association. Owners of other houses the builder has constructed often are better sources. You can ask them if their home required any extra work after they moved in and how the builder responded to complaints.

Schedule regular inspections throughout all stages of construction. Carefully read your building contract beforehand, and act quickly in case of

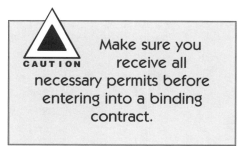

problems. A new home may take a year or two to "settle," which can mean anything from sticking windows and doors to electrical and plumbing problems. Implied warranties generally cover repair of serious structural defects incurred within the first year or two. Warranties offered by the builder often are designed more to protect the company from liability more than for your rights as owner.

Hiring a builder, choosing the plans, purchasing the property and closely monitoring the progress of construction all take time. A contract may or may not include deadlines. Once the builder acquires a certificate of occupancy, you will need to inspect your home and submit a checklist of finishing touches the builder needs to take care of. Then it is time to close the loan and take ownership of your new home.

Your choice of new homes may be between a custom-designed home or a tract house. For some, building one's own home is the ultimate dream. To make sure it does not become a nightmare, check local regulations for minimum lot size and road frontage, as well as availability of water, sewer, electric and gas service.

Suburban developments often show several tract home models, with options ranging from choice of location to amenities such as a pool or bay window. A model may not satisfy all your desires or help you stand out from a cookie-cutter row of neighboring homes, but it would likely cost less than designing and building a home to custom specifications. And, rather than just reviewing a set of blueprints, you have the advantage of seeing the actual finished product, or at least a similar one, before you buy.

Buying an older home

The opposite route is to buy a "handy man's special" or "do-it-yourself fixer-upper," usually older property priced low because it needs repair. This type of purchase can yield a prosperous return or cause nightmarish debt.

If you have proven home improvement skills, a fixer-upper may be the right move for you. You may uncover a palace from an often older, larger structure after only a little work. Older homes often offer more square feet and more cubic feet to work with for remodeling purposes. Some have a distinct character or an antique mystique which owners cherish. In general, they tend to be more centrally located and, in established neighborhoods, property taxes are lower.

> **E-Z TIP**
> Consult a professional inspector to uncover potential problems. Then hire an appraiser to estimate the home's current value and its projected value after improvements.

On the other hand, you can unexpectedly encounter a series of expensive repairs which cannot be ignored. Serious repairs often involve the foundation, plumbing, electricity, or termites. Superficial repairs such as new paint or landscaping are far less expensive and can be put off until you have the time and money. Practical renovations, such as remodeling the kitchen, adding bedrooms or a family room, or installing low-maintenance siding, gain back the most resale value.

> **HOT spot**
> Be aware that the average home-improvement loan carries a much higher interest rate than a mortgage.

Adding on

Often buyers look for homes with expansion potential. A finished basement, porch or attic may become a valuable addition. This is of particular importance in two bedroom homes, which often have limited market appeal and often can be hard to sell. Major home improvements must be weighed as investments; if you add a pool or an expensive garage, you may not get the money back when you resell.

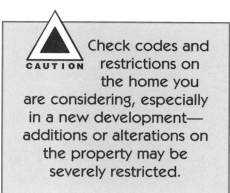

CAUTION Check codes and restrictions on the home you are considering, especially in a new development—additions or alterations on the property may be severely restricted.

Condominiums

Condominiums can be less expensive and save time and money spent on maintenance. In addition, they often provide shared amenities you might not get from a single-family home, such as a pool, health spa, clubhouse and tennis courts. Sometimes you may be required to pay membership fees to use these facilities. You also pay fees for maintenance, renovation and security. Be sure you can live with the rules and regulations of the community. Some ban pets, work vehicles, and even motorcycles. Others restrict your ability to rent the unit.

A condominium be an owned apartment, townhouse, villa, patio home, etc. You also own a share of common property such as a pool, laundry room,

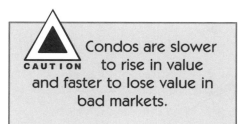

CAUTION Condos are slower to rise in value and faster to lose value in bad markets.

and elevator. A condominium building or development has a board of directors to manage monthly maintenance and security fees and to create and enforce rules. Every state has a specific body of law by which all condominiums must abide. Buyers must meet strict requirements and live with serious restrictions. Weeding out potentially unruly neighbors may help to maintain property values, but it also narrows the market when you decide to sell.

Townhouses often provide as much interior space as a single-family home and usually have at least two floors. But yard space is limited, and a thin wall is all that separates you from your next door neighbor, so be sure you can peacefully coexist.

Mobile homes

Despite their name, most mobile homes are never moved from their original plot. Prices for manufactured homes are typically one-third of a home built on-site. You may select from existing models within a community or have one custom-made. Most come with built-in furnishings. Financing is usually arranged by the manufacturer or developer. Generally, interest rates are two to three points higher than conventional mortgages and terms are shorter.

> **HOT spot** Be sure to select a quality builder; unlike single-family homes, manufactured (mobile) homes are not subject to local building codes.

You may place a mobile home on land you either own or rent. Familiarize yourself with the atmosphere, rules and turnover rate of the community. Even if you are renting land and get in a dispute with ownership, you may have no choice but to sell or move. This can be an expensive and risky ordeal, costing thousands of dollars and potentially causing serious structural damage to your home.

Gated or not gated?

Until recently, gated developments were only found in retirement or upscale communities. Not any longer. Gated communities are increasingly popular. Home buyers prefer the feeling of the added security. In addition, crime rates are often lower in gated communities.

For these reasons, many communities are retrofitting their entries with automatic gate access systems. Unwanted traffic is greatly reduced or even eliminated. The installation of access control and gates upgrades the community from just another subdivision to a "Gated Community" and this usually increases the property values in the community.

There are some drawbacks, however. If your community is also guarded, you pay extra for that service as well and the fees can be considerable. Gates also have the stigma of a community striving to keep itself segregated from its surrounding neighbors. This can lead to some friction in an area where income discrepancy is great. In addition, some people may be more lax in home security, feeling the gates should do all the work. Living behind gates may or may not be for you, but the trend is definitely increasing.

Buying foreclosure property

With a little investigating, you may discover bargain properties not listed by an agent. Owners facing foreclosure often sell their homes for the cost of the equity they've invested. You may still get a bargain at a foreclosure auction or from a lender who wants to unload a foreclosed property. You can often obtain information about foreclosure properties from the county recorder of deeds, legal newspapers, private newsletters, local real estate attorneys, real estate agents and title insurance officers. Common reasons for foreclosure sales include probate, IRS tax seizure, divorce, death or illness, unemployment and property tax sales, along with abandoned, condemned, distressed and run-down properties. Diligent title search and thorough inspection are essential when buying distressed properties.

Owning a multi-family home

Are you considering becoming a landlord? A rental property with proven rental history can be an excellent investment, providing steady income, free rent and large capital appreciation—all with surprisingly little capital invested. Small income properties with two to four apartments can be financed using a residential mortgage with as little as a five percent down payment. You may qualify for a larger mortgage than you would for a single-family home because your potential income would be larger. The lender may require the buyer to live on the property and to have a cash reserve to cover potential rental losses for six months.

> **E-Z TIP**
> In a four-unit building, the rent from three units is often enough to cover monthly mortgage payments, making the landlord's unit rent-free.

When examining rental properties, lenders look for proof of profit from tax returns and a vacancy rate of less than five percent. They also examine operation costs, including maintenance and management. The newer the building, the lower the cost of maintenance. Reasonable maintenance costs range from five percent of gross income for new buildings to 10 percent for older buildings. Professional management companies generally get paid 10 percent of the gross income. A landlord living on the property can help keep maintenance and management costs down and help you qualify you for the loan.

Rental properties can be profitable, but also involve serious risks:

- **Dependence upon rent payments.** Late payments can lead to stress. Vacant units can lead to foreclosure.

- **Declining property value.** Your building may decline in value, especially if income falls and you can't keep up with maintenance costs. This is always a possibility when you have problem tenants or when the neighborhood declines.

- **Slower appreciation.** Multi-family homes generally do not appreciate as rapidly or as much as single-family homes.

- **Limited market.** The buyer's market for multi-family homes is smaller than for single-family homes.

- **Lack of privacy.** You may have to live in the same building with troublesome tenants who have direct access to you. It may be difficult to maintain a business relationship with your tenants.

- **Extensive record-keeping and paperwork.** Depending on the size of the property and the degree of your involvement in everyday operations, it can amount to a full-time job or even a staff of employees.

Finding the right home for you

5

Chapter 5

Finding the right home for your

Finding the right home requires planning, patience and an eye for detail. As an investor, you look for the best value and the most profit potential. As a future resident, you look for a home that best suits your needs and desires. You and your family must thoroughly examine your values and motives for buying a home. This will help you weigh your priorities as you come up with a list of tangibles you would like to see in a home. After assessing your budget and determining the type of home you are interested in, you can narrow your focus and save time by looking only at the properties you want and are able to buy.

Location, location, location

Almost universally, the two most important factors for home buyers are price and location. Once you've determined approximately how much you can afford, you must decide on an area where you would like to live. You must answer a myriad of questions regarding the location of a home:

- *Is the neighborhood safe from crime?* Ask neighbors or local police for their feelings about safety. Seeing a neighborhood at night sometimes shines a new light as well. Unlocked bicycles and open car windows at night are generally signs of a carefree environment. Bars on business windows and screaming sirens indicate a potential crime element. Can you trust that your children and your valuables will be safe?

> **HOT** spot   No single factor has more impact on a home's value than location.

- *Do you like the personal feel of the neighborhood?* Does it reflect your own values and personality? Perhaps you know some friends or co-workers who live there, or have said good things about it. You can meet neighbors at P.T.A. meetings, a local church, or by asking the owner to introduce you to the next door neighbor.

- *Is the local property value holding steady?* Even if the house you are viewing seems like a good deal, an undesirable neighborhood can seriously lower the property value. If the home is more expensive than most others in the neighborhood, it may not hold its resale value. Abandoned buildings or decrepit neighboring houses are bad signs, while home improvements are positive signs.

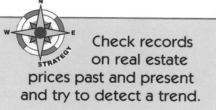

Check records on real estate prices past and present and try to detect a trend.

Changes in property value can result from fluctuating crime rates or changes affecting the area, such as the building of park or a nuclear power plant. You may find out about projected changes from the planning commission.

- *How far are you willing to commute?* If you do commute, are you near the highway, subway or train station you will be using? If you and your spouse will be working permanently in different parts of town, try to find a convenient midway location. Work proximity may not be a factor. You may travel to a different worksite every day, or prefer to live close to friends or recreational or entertainment attractions.

- *What school district is most desirable?* If you have school-aged children, this may be a very important factor in your decision. Are any parks, libraries or other interests nearby? Will your kids have companions in their age group to play with?

> *note* A quality school zone costs all tax-payers, but also boosts property values.

- *How busy are the roads in the neighborhood?* Heavy traffic creates not only a safety hazard for the children, but also noise and air pollution. Is parking a problem?

- *Are convenient shopping centers nearby?* Will you have to travel miles to pick up groceries, or will living near a shopping center create unwanted traffic congestion?

- *What type of atmosphere do you want to live in?* Do you prefer urban, suburban or rural environs? Do you favor a wooded area or prefer it tree-free? Would you like to live on a corner, in a cul-de-sac, or in the middle of the block? Do you object to living near railroad tracks, an airport, a hill, power lines, or commercial property such as a gas station or a factory?

These are just some of the possible questions. Others will arise according to your own priorities and circumstances.

Listing your needs and desires

Defining your price range and desired location is a good start to your search. Now get more specific. Think about the values and motives you have for owning a home. Recall the things you like and don't like about the houses you have been in.

First come up with a list of your needs. These are features you cannot or will not live without. An efficient heating and cooling system, safe and dependable electrical wiring, a sturdy, leak-proof roof, and good plumbing should be first on everyone's list of needs. Then there are more personal needs. Do you need a big backyard for your Doberman or a garage to store your vintage automobile? Maybe you have four growing children who each need their own bedroom.

Desires are features that you would appreciate but that are not critical to your purchase. Perhaps you would like an eat-in kitchen, a bay window or a deck. Maybe you have a special connection to a specific style of house, such as split level, ranch or colonial. Secondary concerns likely will become less important as your home hunt progresses.

HOT spot Keep in mind that you may move again in the future. Records across the U.S. indicate families move once every four years.

Deciding on the right home requires the ability to compromise and prioritize in order to stay within your budget and get the home that's right for you.

Taking a tour

When you have selected several homes you would like to see, bring a map to mark locations and a pen and notebook or tape recorder to take down your initial observations so you can review them later. Ask questions. Get a feel for what it would be like to live there. Does it have a logical, practical layout for your needs?

Write down the room measurements and draw out a basic layout so you can determine if your furniture will fit.

Looking at a prospective home generates a wide range of emotions. Take your emotions into account, but don't let them take over. Agents and sellers feed off prospective buyers' reactions and use them to influence your decision and weaken your negotiating position later on. Reflect on your visit. If you are interested, arrange a second visit and compile a list of questions about the property.

If your first visit was during the day, try for a night showing, or vice versa. Different lighting can expose things that had gone unnoticed, such as cracks in the plaster. Ask the seller your questions, paying special attention to facial expressions and voice inflections.

An owner's situation or attitude can indicate how negotiations might proceed. If you discover the seller is close to bankruptcy, in the process of a divorce or a long-distance move, he or she may be ready for a quick sale. You can also get a good deal if you overlook a seller's sloppiness that does not affect the permanent condition of

HINT

No one knows the house inside and out like the owners; they can answer your questions most accurately—not always by what they say, but by how they say it.

the home but does scare away other sellers. By the same token, don't get drawn in by a big screen TV, an afghan rug or an exquisite art collection if it is not included in the sale.

What to watch out for

Once you make an offer on a home, your lender will likely require you to schedule a professional inspection and appraisal before your loan can be approved. But with a discriminating eye, you can catch the more obvious problems before it gets to that stage. Here are some important points to look for when visiting a home:

Exterior evaluation

- **Style**: Do you like the style and does it fit in with other homes in the area?

- **Foundation**: Loose bricks or uneven or corroded mortar joints can spell trouble.

- **Siding**: Looking at the house from the corners, can you detect bulges in the siding? That probably means foundation or moisture problems.

- **Doors and windows**: Open and inspect each of them. If they stick, reasons may range from fresh paint to poor installation and swelling to a bad foundation. Spongy wood trim will need replacement. Leaky sealing, sticky weather-stripping and broken springs are common problems.

- **Roof**: Tattered shingles may forecast leakage if not fixed; sagging may require major repair. Most real estate agreements include a roof inspection clause, which makes the seller responsible for up to three percent of the purchase price for repairs to correct leaks or replace any damages. If damages exceed that amount and the buyer refuses to pay the excess, the seller has the right to cancel the contract.

- **Chimneys**: Check for solid foundation and flashing between the siding and the chimney.

- **Decks and porches**: Make sure foundations, floors, steps and roofs are solid.

- **Garage**: Are exterior buildings, such as garages, sheds and gazebos attractive and in good condition? They may provide plenty of storage space, but are they practical for your needs? Put them through the same evaluation steps as the home.

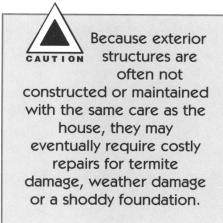

Because exterior structures are often not constructed or maintained with the same care as the house, they may eventually require costly repairs for termite damage, weather damage or a shoddy foundation.

- **Landscaping**: Homeowners can take considerable pride in caring for the lawn. Did the owner manicure the perfect yard, or is it more like an unexplored jungle? Do the trees, shrubs and grass appear healthy? Do gutters and sump pumps drain excess water adequately? Paved sidewalks and driveways can be nice luxuries if they are in good shape.

Interior evaluation

- **Basement/crawl space**: Crawl space floors should be 80 percent covered with plastic to allow a minimal flow of moisture. This prevents dry rot and standing water, which causes structure problems along with mold and mildew buildup.

- **Design**: Take everyday activities into consideration to determine how practical the layout is. How many rooms will you pass through when carrying groceries to the kitchen, trash outside, or laundry from the washroom to the bedroom? Is there ample closet space, especially in the bedroom and near the bathroom? Are bathrooms conveniently located? Considering door and window placement, will your furniture fit? Do you like the overall feel of the house?

- **Floors and floor coverings**: Do they bubble, creek or sag under your feet? Sometimes carpet can be hiding a beautiful wood floor. Is the wood floor, carpet or vinyl stained or worn? Is the carpet pad springy? You shouldn't notice any seams, bubbling, curling or yellowing on vinyl tile.

- **Interior doors**: Do they open, close and lock easily?

- **Walls**: See if the walls bow or are covered with nail holes.

- **Ceilings**: If they appear uneven or discolored, they could require serious structural repair.

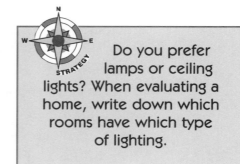

Do you prefer lamps or ceiling lights? When evaluating a home, write down which rooms have which type of lighting.

- **Insulation**: Proper insulation can save lots of money on energy bills. Insulation is judged by its ability to stop heat loss and becomes less effective as it gets older.

- **Attic**: Check for water leaks or bowed rafters.

- **Appliances**: Does the house come with the appliances you need? Or will the ones you own fit? Test out the dishwasher, stove, garbage disposal and other appliances. Buyer's insurance often protects appliances for a year.

- **Pest control**: Obtain an insect inspection test, which is often free, to determine any infestation or damage. Most real estate agreements include a termite inspection clause. This makes the seller responsible for up to three percent of the purchase price for treatment and repair of infestation and damage by termites or any wood boring insect. If damages exceed that amount and the buyer refuses to pay the excess, the seller has the right to cancel the contract.

- **Air conditioning**: How old and in what condition is the air conditioning unit? Check to see that it operates properly.

- **Heating**: What type of heating system does the house use? Find out which rooms have vents and make sure they work. If the house's only heat source is a wood stove, you may have trouble obtaining a mortgage. It also may be a safety concern if you have young children.

E-Z TIP
Take a good look at the attic. Could you expand your living space by finishing a room in the attic or could you use the space for storage?

- **Plumbing**: Detect any leaks. Make sure fixtures operate adequately. Check the water pressure by flushing the toilet and running the sinks at the same time. Run the shower on hot for 15 to 20 minutes to test the water heater.

- **Electricity**: Check to see that all outlets work. If the circuit breaker panel is less than 100 amp, or 200 amp if the house has electric heat or an electric stove, you could have problems.

Showing your home

If you are selling, does your home appear to be a good value compared to other homes in the same price range? First impressions are pivotal. A home that "shows well" commands more money and sells more quickly. Here are some quick-fix improvements to make your home more attractive:

Outside

Begin with the outside of your home. What impression does it make? Instead of painting the entire exterior or replacing the siding, consider these inexpensive and easy improvements:

- repaint the front door and polish or replace the door handle

- reseal and paint the driveway

- clean and lubricate the garage door

- manicure shrubs, trees, lawn and replace plants as needed

- add new mulch and remove weeds

- repair or replace any damaged roof tiles, shingles, bricks or gutters

- resurface areas where there is cracked or peeling paint

- repair damaged or missing caulking

- wash the windows

- replace anything outside your home that is obviously loose, hanging, decaying or warped

Inside

Consider the interior: When potential buyers enter your home, what is the first thing they see? Is it a high-traffic hallway, alcove or foyer? If so, be sure this area is clean. Try brightening with fresh or artificial flowers. Also, made sure that the house is well lit. In addition:

Many real estate agents suggest opening all blinds, shutters and window treatments. This allows the maximum amount of light to enter and the home seems warmer, brighter and more welcoming.

- replace any cracked or broken windows

- shampoo the carpet

- repair peeling wallpaper and chipped paint

- make sure all locks work and all hinges operate smoothly

- check doorbell, chimes and alarm system

- remove mildew and stains from the bathroom

- clean and degrease the kitchen

- remove clutter and unnecessary furniture to make the home seem larger

- check the water pressure in faucets

- repair clogged drains

- be sure all light switches work

- service heating and cooling equipment

- wash your car if you are going to leave it in the driveway

- remove any indications of your political or religious beliefs

note Most experts feel the cost of major renovation does not pay if its purpose is to sell your home.

The above are simple, relatively inexpensive things that can be done to spruce up your home. But what about the big things? Although there may be things that need fixing, they do not necessarily have to be fixed by you. Only fix something if you can recoup the money from the buyer or if it will actually add to the perceived value of your home. The price can always be adjusted downward to reflect needed repairs, but adding the cost of repairs can easily price a home out of the market.

Full disclosure

In most states, if the seller of real property knows of a material defect that could not be reasonably discovered by the buyer, there is a legal obligation to disclose that defect to the buyer. If the defect is open and obvious, then the seller has no such obligation to do so. If you had no knowledge of the defect, then you have no liability. You may not hide environmental problems such as asbestos and urea formaldehyde insulation, illegal construction or alterations that violate codes, rezoning plans, neighborhood construction, or crimes which occurred in the house, any of which could affect price and desirability.

Do not deceive the buyer. Assume the buyer will ultimately discover every defect you try to hide and will do so prior to settlement day. Do not risk having the buyer renege on the deal, demand further monetary concessions for your failure to disclose, or sue you for fraudulent misrepresentation.

Discrimination

If, as a member of a racial or ethnic minority in the market to buy or sell a home, you have been discriminated against, your rights may be protected by the Fair Housing Law (Title VIII of the Civil Rights Act of 1968, amended in 1974 and 1989). It aims to prevent discrimination in the selling, renting and financing of housing by real estate professionals. The law does not apply to private individuals who own three or fewer single-family homes as long as:

• no real estate agent is used

• the advertising does not use discriminatory language

• the owner has sold no more than one home (not including a primary residence) in a two-year span

The Fair Housing Law states that no agent or lender may:

- deny you the right to buy, rent or view a home based on your race, color, national origin, religion, sex, or disability, or because you have children under 18

- urge owners to sell by saying that minorities are moving into the neighborhood

- use discriminating factors to determine the terms or conditions of a mortgage

If you believe you are a victim of discrimination, take the following steps:

- make a record of each meeting or phone call, including the person's name and title, the place, time and date each meeting occurred, and a detailed account of what happened

- keep applications, receipts, business cards and all documents relevant to your case

- demand an explanation from your agent, then go to his or her employer

If your problems continue, you can write to the national, state or local fair-housing enforcement agency. You can write to Fair Housing Division, U.S. Department of Housing and Urban Development (HUD), 451 7th St., S.W., Washington, D.C., 20410-5500, or call toll-free 800-669-9777. State and local agencies will be faster; they must begin proceedings within 30 days. If you appeal to the U.S. District Court or state or local courts, you must do so within 180 days of the incident.

Financing your home

Chapter 6

Financing your home

What you'll find in this chapter:

- Different types of lenders
- The types of mortgages
- The adjustable rate mortgage
- Creative home financing techniques
- Borrowing considerations

You must choose from a variety of home mortgages and from a number of different lenders. If you need to take out a loan, first evaluate your goals. For instance, if you feel you will be moving again in a few years, aim for a loan with a low down payment; if you plan to stay put a while, go for the lowest interest rates. You can find mortgage information from your real estate agent, bank, newspaper, or yellow pages. Diligent mortgage comparison shopping can help you trim your monthly payments and save thousands of dollars over the life of your mortgage.

Types of lenders

The four basic mortgage lenders are:

1) **Large banks.** Traditional lenders are mainly large banks. These have the strictest requirements and qualifying formulas but often the lowest interest rates.

2) ***Credit unions and hometown banks.*** These are more progressive than traditional banks. In addition to past financial history, they take into account your current financial situation, present ability to pay and your financial stability.

DEFINITION

3) ***Mortgage brokers.*** *Mortgage brokers* are financial matchmakers between lending institutions and qualified borrowers, and they closely resemble both traditional and more progressive lenders. They represent banks, organizations and private individuals with money to lend. About half of all mortgages are handled by mortgage brokers. However, with their expertise and convenience comes a fee for finding you a loan.

4) ***Government agencies.*** The Federal Housing Authority (FHA) and the Veteran's Administration (VA) are the two chief lenders. The FHA and the VA are actually insurers, not lenders. They guarantee your loan (or part of the loan) in case you default. If you qualify, you may obtain an FHA guaranteed loan for as little as five percent down payment. Although you can obtain a VA mortgage with no downpayment, VA mortgages are only available to qualifying veterans. To find out if you qualify for an FHA or VA mortgage, contact a real estate agent, your local bank, credit union, the VA or the FHA.

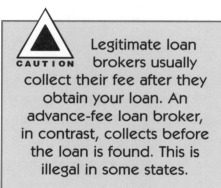

CAUTION Legitimate loan brokers usually collect their fee after they obtain your loan. An advance-fee loan broker, in contrast, collects before the loan is found. This is illegal in some states.

State financing agencies provide low-interest home financing through mortgage revenue bonds. These are Housing and Urban Development (HUD) supervised programs that require applicants to be non-homeowners during the previous three years.

Types of mortgages

Lenders use sliding scale formulas to determine your interest rate, down payment, points and monthly payments. They also consider your credit history; the better it is, the better the rates you'll receive (see page 16). You can choose a mortgage with fixed or variable interest rates and payment intervals.

note

Mortgage ads often use a variety of deceptive rates, but only the annual percentage rate (APR) factors in all costs of borrowing money with a fixed-rate loan, including interest rate, points and closing costs. Federal law requires the lender to supply you with a "Truth in Lending Disclosure" estimate, which includes APR, three days after you apply for a loan. Other factors to consider are early and late payment terms and refinancing options.

Here are the basic types of mortgages:

1) **Conventional mortgages** feature fixed interest rates and fixed monthly payments, typically over a 30-year span. Most buyers like the predictability of fixed, regular payments. If you qualify, and if you can afford monthly payments 15 to 25 percent higher than a 30-year mortgage, you might consider a 15- or 20-year loan. This may save you over 50 percent in total interest over the life of the mortgage. Biweekly payments are another way of shortening the life of a loan. Typically, these involve a fee for automatically deducting payments from your bank account or paycheck.

2) **Adjustable rate mortgages (ARMs)** offer an initial interest rate of at least a point or two lower than a conventional mortgage. The rate is tied to a market index and changes at regular intervals, usually every year.

> **HINT**
> If you plan to take out an ARM, insist on an interest rate cap, typically limiting hikes to two percentage points per year and five to six points over the life of the mortgage.

With an ARM, the buyer shoulders the risk of changing interest rates, which are unpredictable even to the experts. Some adjustable-rate mortgages allow you the option of locking in a low interest rate or refinancing after a specified period of time has elapsed, usually for a fee. Rollover mortgages feature interest rates which are adjusted every three to five years to meet current market trends.

3) **Balloon mortgages** require you to pay large lump sums at fixed intervals, usually every one to seven years, in addition to regular monthly payments. These payments can shorten the life of the mortgage considerably, but the large payments can strain finances.

4) **Graduated payment mortgages (GPMs)** feature monthly payments which are low initially, then increase over the life of the mortgage. This allows buyers to purchase more expensive homes than they could afford with a conventional mortgage, offering the promise of increased income in a several years down the road.

DEFINITION

However, if you cannot make the payments and are forced to sell after only a few years, you may suffer financial catastrophe known as *negative amortization*. This means that even after years of regular monthly payments, you still owe money on interest and have failed to make a dent in the loan principal.

5) **Reverse annuity mortgages** involve using the equity in a home to purchase an annuity from which monthly interest is paid.

6) **Shared appreciation mortgages (SAMs)** allow the lender to obtain an ownership interest in the property at a certain date and according to specific conditions set forth in the mortgage document.

7) Various **state and federal government programs** offer mortgages. For instance, the Community Home Buyer's Program (CHBP) from Federal National Mortgage Association (Fannie Mae) is

for families with a household income not exceeding 115 percent of the median in your area. Payments can be up to 33 percent of your income, with as little as five percent down payment (or three percent with up to a two percent gift or grant). The usual two month's mortgage reserve due at closing is waived. The Department of Housing and Urban Development (HUD) and Federal Homeowner's Association, plus other state and federal programs, also offer assistance in obtaining mortgages.

Creative home financing techniques

Sometimes obtaining a mortgage can be difficult, especially if you are a first-time buyer, self-employed or have a poor credit history. One of these alternative home financing techniques might work for you:

- *Seller financing.* The seller holds the deed and receives payments from the buyer. In case of default, the seller can foreclose on the home. Coupled with the risk of irregular payments and default, the seller does enjoy several potential benefits: a larger pool of qualified buyers, more negotiating power and a better return. The seller also has the opportunity to defer tax on profit from the sale.

note | Lease option payments are non-refundable and credited to the purchase price.

- *Lease option buying.* One way to initiate a potential sale is through a lease option. It gives the tenant a right to become comfortable with the house before committing with a big downpayment, and gives the owner immediate monthly income. The option to buy often occurs in six months to two years, and has two payment obligations: a lump sum, typically three to five percent of the price of the house, and a monthly amount—usually $50 to $300—paid in addition to rent.

- *Equity sharing.* This arrangement demands an attorney because it involves complex legal considerations. An investor buys and finances a home. You agree to occupy the home and pay the mortgage through a rental fee. You also maintain the home and agree to live in the home for a specified period of time, at the end of which you can sell the home. Once the home is sold, you reimburse the investor his initial contribution and divide the remaining profit between you. The investor knows you will take care of the home because you have an equity stake in it. You also receive part of the profits and deduct the interest portion of your mortgage payments, as well as your share of the property taxes from your income taxes.

- *Co-signers.* If your credit is less than favorable, perhaps you can convince family or friends to guarantee your loan. Be careful, however, since if you default, your co-signer becomes responsible for the loan. Many banks eagerly accept a co-signer, because they then have someone financially stable to sue in case of default.

- *Pension plan borrowing.* Your pension or profit-sharing plan can lend you money based upon your contribution to the plan. The law allows you to borrow up to one-half the vested amount (your money in the plan) or $50,000, whichever is less. A plan can lend up to $10,000, regardless of the vested amount. If the loan is to purchase a principal residence, no term limit will be imposed upon the loan.

> **HOT spot** If you borrow from your pension plan and die or retire before the full amount of the loan is repaid, the outstanding balance will be deducted from your estate.

- *Life insurance.* You can borrow against the cash or surrender value of a wholesale life or permanent life insurance policy. Many policies allow you to borrow up to 95 percent of its value, with no time limit to repay. But remember, your coverage under a policy is reduced by the amount you borrow. Outstanding balances and interest are deducted from any distributions under the policy should you die.

- *Inheritance buy-outs.* If your inheritance is held in trust or otherwise won't be available until later, you can sell rights to your inheritance or trust to companies that can wait for the funds to be released.

- *Syndicates.* Organize a group for the purpose of investing in real estate secured by your mortgage. Investors also receive equity or profits from the home.

- *Probate properties.* These are unwanted homes inherited by people who would prefer to sell them and pocket the money. The prospects of regular monthly income may motivate these owners to settle with little or no cash down.

note
Heirs are usually busy people and can be highly motivated sellers, especially if mortgage payments must be made on time.

- *Union financing.* Some unions offer first-time home loans to members who pay as little as three percent down with no loan origination fees. Parents and children of union members also may qualify.

Negotiating a sale and closing

7

Chapter 7

Negotiating a sale and closing

> ## What you'll find in this chapter:
>
> ⟹ What to ask the seller
>
> ⟹ Making your offer stand out
>
> ⟹ Protecting your rights with a sales contract
>
> ⟹ Checklist for a complete home appraisal
>
> ⟹ Avoiding hidden costs

If the home passes your inspection and you are still interested, it is time to make an offer.

"Everything is negotiable"

Consider what you are willing to pay and what you want the sale to include. Many buyers who work without an agent fail to realize the fact that almost everything is negotiable.

Sellers pad the asking price between five and 10 percent, knowing they probably won't get full price. However, an offer of less than 90 percent of the asking price may insult the seller and make him reluctant to deal with you. If a seller remains firm on the asking price, perhaps you can bargain for appliances, repairs, or help with closing costs.

Finding out how long the home has been on the market can be critical. In a fast market, a well-priced home will receive several bids within a week or two. If a home has been for sale over six months, the seller is obviously asking too much, or you may uncover the same serious problems with the home as others before you.

The seller, or his agent, is not obligated to reveal motivation. But saying you must know in order to "meet the needs of the seller" usually shows enough diplomacy to produce an honest answer.

Motivation, usually defined by time or price limitations, is equally critical. Try to conceal your motivation while finding out the seller's. For instance, you may have just sold your home and be in a hurry to settle. But letting the seller know this will only make him more firm on the price. On the other hand, the seller may be relocating to a job out of town and not have much time to haggle over price.

Other bargaining tactics involve real or contrived competition. A seller may say another buyer is ready to purchase for a higher price. A buyer may mention another house with more features for the same cost. You must be shrewd enough to avoid being manipulated or involved in a bidding war, but still get what you want. Don't become vulnerable or grow too attached to the property. If the seller provides you with no alternative, look for another home.

Hiring a real estate attorney

At this point, it may be wise to hire a real estate attorney who specializes in your market. This may cost between $300 and $1,000, depending on the level of service you wish to receive, but can provide you with insurance against costly mistakes or misunderstandings. An attorney can review the sales contract and closing documents, negotiate amendments and attachments, clarify conditions of approval, and act as a liaison in case of dispute or delay.

Making an offer

An Offer to Purchase Real Estate form outlines the proposed terms of the sale. Specifically, it:

- names the agent and commission to be paid

- is contingent upon satisfactory appraisal, inspection and clear title

- designates the amount due upon signing the sales agreement and the total purchase price

- provides a timetable for the number of days the buyer has to:

- obtain a mortgage as detailed

- inspect the home

- make a sales agreement

- close on the home

> *note*
> An accepted offer effectively takes the home off the market.

If contingencies are not met, you have several options: withdraw your offer, have problems repaired, or have the price adjusted.

DEFINITION

To prove your interest is serious, you should accompany the offer with a *good faith* deposit, usually a percent of the property's total price. This "earnest money" should be held in escrow and refunded after a certain number of days if the offer expires or is withdrawn. On the check, write "trustee" or "fiduciary agent" after the name.

Keep in mind that the owner may receive multiple offers. To make your offer stand out, you can:

- offer more than the listing price (most other bids will be below or at best match the listing price)

- offer to pay some of the owner's expenses, such as title, appraisal or survey fees

- be flexible with closing date

- offer more earnest money

- show documented proof of mortgage prequalification

- limit escape clauses

If owner is hesitant to include an item you want in the sale price, offer to negotiate a price for it separately.

Once the seller receives the offer, he may reject it, accept it as is, or submit a counter offer proposing certain changes. You may haggle over altering the price, including extra items such as a satellite dish or an antique hutch, revising the closing date, or excluding certain provisions. The fewer concessions the buyer asks for beyond those of the offering agreement, the quicker negotiations will proceed. Too many changes can cause the seller to lose patience and cancel the contract altogether. Agreed upon revisions must be initialed by both parties.

The sales contract

Once you reach a compromise, it is time to draw up a sales contract, also called an Agreement to Sell Real Estate. To protect your rights and ensure you include all necessary provisions, have your attorney review it.

The contract states the purchase price, deposit, mortgage interest rate and estimated closing costs, along with the agent's commission and a statement that all utility and insurance bills will be prorated at the time of settlement. You should attach a separate "legal description" of the property as it appears in the seller's deed, including the address, survey points, and a detailed description of everything included in the sale price. Disputes often arise over substituted appliances or unwanted items left behind.

Contingency clauses will make the contract subject to satisfactory inspections and appraisal. It will also detail which companies perform the tests, who pays for them, dates by which they should be executed, and what happens if the home does not pass. You should spell out exactly what should be in "working order" at the time of settlement.

> **note**
> Aside from the home passing certain inspections, the seller is not obligated to make any guarantees about future condition of the roof, heating and cooling system, and so on.

Also listed will be the closing date and date the contract expires, usually between 30 and 90 days, depending on the market. The buyer and seller should keep each other informed each step of the process. If unexpected delays occur, you may need to convince the other party to revise certain dates set out in the contract.

Submitting your loan application

As soon as both parties sign the sales contract, it is time to submit your loan application. The lender will spell out in the loan application all information and documentation necessary to process your application. This may include: income tax returns from the last two years, pay stubs, profit-loss statements (if self-employed), the past three to six months' bank statements for all your accounts, car titles, and other proof of income and assets.

During your interview you will:

- fill out a formal application

- pay processing, appraisal, and credit reporting fees, loan discount points and—if you assume a mortgage—a loan-assumption fee

- learn about loan origination fees, usually one percent of the loan, which must be paid prior to approval

- receive a good faith estimate of closing costs within three business days of completing your loan application

- find out if the loan application fee will be refunded should you be rejected

- discover how long the prevailing interest is good for and when it can be locked in

- determine if you need private mortgage insurance or face other special insurance considerations

> **HOT spot** It is illegal for the lender to make purchasing credit life insurance a condition of accepting your application at this time.

Final exams

Before the lender processes the loan application, a number of tests must be scheduled on the home, including appraisal, inspection, title search and survey, plus well water, soil and other environmental tests. Often the lender makes these arrangements for the buyer. However, if the buyer requests specific companies, be sure the lender approves them.

Appraisal

After you have received preliminary loan approval, the lender selects an appraiser to provide an official estimate of the home's market value. Be sure the appraiser is state-certified and MAI approved. The buyer pays the appraisal fee, which can cost from $200 to $350. It may include pictures, a map and a detailed floor plan. In busy markets, it may take over a month. If time is of the essence, you may wish to propose a tiered pricing plan based on how soon the appraisal is completed.

Inspection

The seller typically pays for the inspection, which is usually between $150 and $300. The price will be more for new, old or expensive homes, or if it must be done on a holiday or after hours. Specialists are required to inspect condominiums. The seller must choose a recognized professional who should be certified by the National Institute of Building Inspectors, the American Society of Home Inspectors, or both.

Avoid an inspector who has any vested interest in doing repairs themselves.

Clear title

The seller also typically pays for a title search, which is usually required by the lender. The title company will search all public records at the County Recorder's Office or Registry of Deeds for unpaid taxes, judgments, mortgage payments or mechanic liens. It also looks for third party claims from an ex-spouse, an heir or a business partner. If any marks turn up, the buyer should either cancel the offer or demand they be cleared before proceeding. To protect you against any marks the title search may not uncover, even a clerical error, you should also purchase title insurance. If an encumbrance is discovered after the sale, the title company can satisfy it by claiming part of the seller's proceeds.

Never take title to property unless you are fully aware of its legal condition.

A Quitclaim Deed differs from a warranty deed because it bypasses checks on any encumbrances and does not warranty the property in any way. This type of transaction is common among family members.

Land survey

A survey is particularly important for rural homes. It can verify that the property is within city limits or lies within a particular school district. Also check with the next-door neighbors to make sure there are no informal agreements on land boundaries.

Zoning

Before you get ideas about building on or making changes to the property, obtain a copy of all covenants and restrictions from neighborhood developers and zoning particulars on the property. You may be surprised how strict some codes are.

Well water

note The well's drinking water should be at least 100 feet from the waste water.

If your new home uses well water, have the water quality tested. Be sure to do this before settlement day because it often requires two tests to pass. Find out if the seller has had problems with the septic tank, what shape it is in, and when it was last emptied.

Perk test

If you are considering purchasing land that requires the installation of a septic tank, you must have the soil tested. Often the county will perform this test, which is called a perk test. Since septic tanks are not compatible with all soils and since this test is not required to sell land, you could make a serious mistake if you buy untested land. The sale of the home should be contingent upon this test.

Environmental tests

Two environmental issues that commonly call for completely honest disclosure from the owner are lead paint and radon gas.

- *Lead paint*: Federal law now requires sellers of pre-1978 built homes to tell prospective buyers about any lead-based paint used in or around the property. Many states also require disclosure of information about asbestos and vermin infestation (including termites).

- *Radon Gas*: Radon is a colorless, odorless, radioactive gas resulting from decomposing uranium in the soil. This uranium is not negligently buried but occurs naturally in both rock and soil. Radon gas has been shown to accumulate in inadequately ventilated homes built on such rock or soil. The federal Environmental Protection Agency has found unhealthy levels of radon in every state.

> *note*
>
> Many real estate contracts contain escape clauses if dangerous levels of radon are found.

If dangerous levels of radon are detected and you still want to buy the home, have a radon correction clause inserted into the contract. This makes the sale of the home contingent upon correcting the problem. It is best to have your home tested by an approved professional. Check with your state Environmental Protection Agency for more information about radon testing.

"Cost of ownership" issues

Before purchasing a home, investigate other factors that affect the cost of ownership, including taxes, utilities and insurance.

Taxes

High taxes can make a property unaffordable. Find out the real estate taxes, which usually are on the listing agent's property data sheet. Double check with the seller and local tax assessor. The seller may also have a lower rate because of some type of tax abatement, sometimes given to senior citizens, veterans and certain religious organization members. Or the owner may be paying a higher rate to pay an overdue utility bill or some other penalty. Also check the schedule for property tax payment. It may be due at the end of the fiscal year or before the upcoming tax year.

note

In some areas, your tax rate may change once the home changes ownership and your house is assessed for tax purposes.

Utilities

Does the house use natural gas or oil? Oil tanks buried underground can be an expensive headache if codes or laws require their removal. Sometimes grandfather regulations can protect you against this burden. Obtain records of utility bills—such as water, sewer, and garbage removal—and factor them into the overall cost of the home.

Insurance

Homeowner's insurance must be purchased prior to settlement. It should be dated as of the settlement date and the lender must be named beneficiary.

HOT spot
While you need only cover the amount of the mortgage, consider the replacement value of your home in the event it is destroyed by fire.

Depending upon the geographical location, you may also be required to purchase natural disaster insurance including flood, earthquake and hurricane insurance.

Insurance packages start with HO(homeowner's)-1, which covers hazard damages including fire, wind,

If you use one company to cover all your insurance needs, such as home, auto and life, you will probably save on your total bill, and save time by paying for everything at once.

explosions, smoke, broken windows along with burglary, vandalism and liability. HO-2 also covers plumbing, heating and electricity. Condominiums and townhouse units can be insured by HO-6. You can lower your rates by taking on a deductible. If you have a $500 deductible, a repair less than that amount—such as a broken window or a bicycle theft—will come out of your pocket.

Neighborhood perks and fees

Certain developments charge mandatory membership fees—and even more to use perks that may attract you like the pool, tennis court or health spa.

Letter of Commitment

This letter from the lender guarantees you have been approved to buy the home. When you receive this letter be sure to read it carefully. You must check for errors or misunderstandings as it will outline all of the terms and conditions of the loan. If you are satisfied, sign the letter, make copies for yourself and return it to the lender.

Federal law entitles you to see a Uniform Settlement Statement, which officially lists all costs associated with the purchase, a day before settlement. If the home is financed with an FHA-approved mortgage or is FHA-insured, you must use a HUD Settlement Statement. This approved form is available from the title or closing agent.

Pre-settlement walk-through

Prior to settlement you should inspect your new home to make sure everything that is supposed to be there is, that all repairs have been made, and that everything is in working order. Be sure to schedule your walk-through at a time of day when you have enough light to examine the grounds and outside of the home. Any last-minute changes must be reflected in your payments on settlement day.

Settlement

Settlement, also called closing, involves the formal exchange of title and the signing of various documents. The buyer must inform the seller of the time and place to attend. Other interested parties who may attend include agents, attorneys, the closing agent and or title agent.

The seller is responsible for bringing:

- deed, title, and keys to the home

- inspection reports

- bills that will be transferred, such as property tax, insurance policies

- bill of sale for personal property, etc.

The buyer must bring the purchase contract along with checks to pay some or all of the following:

- down payment to the lender

- deposit for prepaid taxes and insurance to the escrow agent

- real estate agent's commission

- attorney's fees

- fees for survey, tax transfer, appraisal, notary, title search, and lender's attorney

Closing documents

At settlement, the buyer may receive a stack of documents to sign. Ideally, you should examine any document you have not already read, or have your attorney review them. Some common documents you may encounter are:

1) **Warranty deed**. Make sure it is made out exactly as you requested. It is called a warranty deed because the seller guarantees he or she has the right to transfer title free of any defects. Some states call these deeds bargain and sale deeds, grant deeds, special warranty deeds or security deeds. The deed should be recorded in the County Recorder's Office or the Registry of Deeds.

   All names must be spelled correctly. If there will be another name on your deed, one name should be followed by one of these terms:

   - *tenant in common*: two or more parties own and have equal interest in the same property

   - *joint tenant with right of survivorship*: same as above but survivor inherits entire property

   - *tenancy by the entirety*: limited to husband and wife who own the property, as one, with survivorship, but neither spouse can sell his/her interest (not legal in every state)

These terms establish exactly what will happen to the property in the event of your death. In addition, be sure the property you are buying is accurately represented with the correct legal description.

2) **Mortgage note**. This note secures the loan and outlines the specific conditions of your mortgage loan. Since it will include repayment terms, be sure you fully understand them as this note becomes legally binding once you sign it. By signing this document, you give the lender a lien on the property. If you sign a deed of trust instead of a mortgage, title is not conveyed to the lender, only the right to have the property sold in the event of default. Both the mortgage and a deed of trust should be recorded in the County Recorder's Office or the Registry of Deeds.

3) **Quitclaim deed**. If any title problems arise at the closing, these often can be handled with a quitclaim deed, whereby the person signing such a deed cedes his or her rights to the property.

4) **Affidavit**. Either buyer or seller—or both—may be asked to sign an affidavit swearing the property is free of liens, judgments, assessments or other encumbrances.

Moving into your new home

Moving can be a time of excitement, stress and confusion. Here are a few pointers to help things go more smoothly:

- *Change of address notices.* When it is time to move, mail or fax a Change of Address Notice to all your professional and personal contacts, at least two weeks in advance if possible. The post office usually has its own form.

- *Take inventory of your possessions.* Keep in mind the moving company will charge per 100 pounds. Make a list of all your possessions to guard against theft or misplacement; a video-taped inventory is even better proof. Now may be a good time to part with that heavy antique hutch, your baseball card collection, or a slew of clothes you no longer wear. Why not hold a garage sale? Advertise it with street posters and in the local paper. Offer everything left the afternoon of the last day of sale at half price, and donate the rest to charity.

- *Moving companies and packing.* Before committing to a moving company, get at least three estimates. Find out exactly what their insurance covers and if you would pay a deductible. Movers don't take credit cards; you will have to pay in cash. You may decide to save money by renting a truck and moving yourself, perhaps with the help of friends and family. But is it worth the risk and hassle? That depends on how far you are moving and what you will bring. Pack separately in your car things you'll need immediately, such as toiletries and several days' change of clothes, plus valuables such as jewelry and important documents.

Make sure all your utilities, including gas, water, electricity and telephone, will be turned on and transferred into your name before you arrive. Find out the location of the water heater, fuse box, and gas and water shutoffs, and also how they operate. Obtain all appliance manuals, warranties and service records. For security purposes, you may decide to change the locks on all exterior doors. Once you move in, post all important phone numbers, and review emergency procedures with the kids. Make sure your home is well lit and secure. Your utility company may conduct a free energy audit and suggest a number of money-saving improvements.

> **HINT** You can save money by doing your own packing. Grocery stores or department stores may give you large, sturdy boxes. But leave breakable items, such as fine china and delicate lamps, for the professionals.

Capitalizing on tax breaks

Chapter 8
Capitalizing on tax breaks

What you'll find in this chapter:

⇒ Taking advantage of tax breaks

⇒ Determining your mortgage terms

⇒ What costs are deductible?

⇒ Learning about the adjusted cost basis

⇒ When a rollover is right for you

Owning a home provides an unbeatable tax shelter. Home-buyers may make tax deductions for mortgage interest, closing costs and home-office use. When it's time to sell, your "adjusted tax basis" may reduce your taxable profit, while special rollover and one-time exclusion clauses may exempt you from paying taxes on your profit. Often, only after purchasing their first home do taxpayers discover the many advantages of itemizing their taxes, which may include deducting charitable contributions, state income taxes and even medical bills.

> **HOT spot** You are responsible for keeping all records, receipts and tax returns for at least seven years after you have sold the house.

At first, it may be wise to hire a tax lawyer or accountant so you can maximize your tax savings. Federal exemptions are complicated and state laws vary considerably.

Mortgage interest

Each year, you can deduct all interest payments on your principal residence from your gross annual income. This can amount to huge savings on your April 15 tax bill, particularly early on in a conventional mortgage when the majority of each payment goes toward paying interest.

With a $100,000, 30-year mortgage at eight percent, in your first year nearly $8,000 of your $8,800 mortgage payments (over 90 percent) will go toward interest. In fact, not until the 22nd year of your mortgage will more of your payment go toward principal than interest—if you own the house that long.

Property taxes

All state and local property taxes are deductible from your taxable income each year you own the home. This is true even if (A) the seller pays for part of your taxes, and (B) if it is not your principal residence.

Closing costs

After paying cash for points, application fees, legal fees, title search, agent commission, and so on, your finances may be nearly drained. But keep in mind you can deduct your closing costs from your gross income, which means you can count on paying even less in taxes. These "acquisition costs," as the IRS calls them, can add up to well over three percent of your home's price.

Moving costs

If your move is based on a job change, you may be eligible to deduct some associated expenses. To qualify, it must be a full-time job at least 50 miles farther away from your old home than your old job. If you were previously unemployed, your new job must be at least 50 miles from your previous residence. If you are self-employed, you must prove you work at least 39 weeks in each of the next two years in the new location.

> *note*
> The IRS allows up to a $1,500 deduction for house-hunting trips and temporary living expenses. There is no maximum deduction for shipping and travel expenses.

Home-office deductions

You may deduct a percentage of your home expenses if you use your home for business. Calculate the percentage, in square feet or by the fraction, of the house you use for business. If you use a 20 by 20 foot room (400 square feet) and your house is 2,000 square feet, you are using 20 percent of the house. If your office takes up one level of three equally-sized floors in your home, you are using 33.3 percent. Use that percent of your yearly mortgage bill to calculate your deductible amount.

Adjusted cost basis

Your home's "adjusted cost basis" accounts for not only associated costs of purchase, but also any special assessments and permanent improvements.

> **HOT** spot
> Minor repairs, redecorating and maintenance are not generally included as improvements. Refer specific questions to your accountant.

This increases the value of your home, which helps reduce your capital gain when you sell. You may have paid a neighborhood fee for installing light posts or a newly paved road. Or you added a sky light in your den. You can include something as minor as a curtain rod.

Rollover

DEFINITION

With the rollover plan, you must first determine the *adjusted basis* of your home. This is calculated by adding the price you paid for the home, plus improvements and minus damages, plus the gain from the sale of a previous home. In the eyes of the IRS, the amount of profit you make on selling your home is the difference between the adjusted basis and the amount you sell the house for. For example, a house with an adjusted basis of $65,000 that you sell for $100,000 realizes a $35,000 profit.

You may postpone paying tax on this profit as long as you replace your principal home within two years and the replacement home is worth at least as much as the amount realized on the sale of your previous residence.

> You can continue to rollover profit from selling your home indefinitely, as long as you purchase replacement homes at least equal to the amount of your sale, and you purchase within two years.

The IRS is absolutely firm on the two year time period, and rollover only applies to your principal residence, not on second homes or other types of property. The rollover deduction has a number of complicated provisions that would allow you to purchase a less expensive home and still meet IRS requirements. You should seek the advice of a qualified real estate professional if you are seeking this deduction.

Gain on sale of principal residence

The new law now allows married couples, filing jointly as homeowners, to exclude a maximum $500,000 in gain from the sale of their principal residence. A single taxpayer may exclude up to $250,000. This law is retroactive to May 7, 1997, and may be used only once every two years. To qualify, the taxpayer must have used the home as a principal residence for at least two of the five years immediately preceding the sale. The effect of this law is to eliminate the need to rollover the capital gains from the sale of the principal residence and allow the homeowner to purchase a less expensive home or even rent.

The forms in this guide

About These Made E-Z Forms:
While the legal forms and documents in this product generally conform to the requirements of courts nationwide, certain courts may have additional requirements. Before completing and filing the forms in this product, check with the clerk of the court concerning these requirements.

NOTICE

While the forms and documents in this guide generally conform to the requirements of courts and real estate boards nationwide, certain courts and realty boards may have additional requirements or may use alternative forms and documents. Before completing and filing any forms or documents in this guide, check with the clerk of the court and the appropriate county board of realty concerning these requirements.

ADDRESS CHANGE NOTICE

Date:

To:

Dear

    Please be advised that effective   ,   (year),
our address has been changed from:

_____

_____

to

_____

_____

    Our new telephone number is:

    Please make note of the above information and direct all correspondence to us at our new address. Thank you.

_____

AGREEMENT TO SELL REAL ESTATE

_____, of
_____ as Seller, and
_____, of
_____ as Buyer, hereby agree that
the Seller shall sell and the Buyer shall buy the following described property UPON THE TERMS AND CONDITIONS HEREINAFTER SET FORTH, which shall include the STANDARDS FOR REAL ESTATE TRANSACTIONS set forth within this contract.

1. LEGAL DESCRIPTION of real estate located in _____
_____ County, State of _____:

2. PURCHASE PRICE _____ Dollars. Method of Payment:

    (a) Deposit to be held in trust by _____ $_____
    (b) Approximate principal balance of first mortgage to which conveyance shall be
        subject, if any, to Mortgage lender:_____ $_____
        Interest _____% per annum: Method of payment _____
    (c) Other: _____ $_____
    (d) Cash, certified or local cashier's check on closing and delivery of deed (or such
        greater or lesser amount as may be necessary to complete payment of purchase
        price after credits, adjustments and prorations). $_____

3. PRORATIONS: Taxes, insurance, interest, rents and other expenses and revenue of said property shall be prorated as of the date of closing.

4. RESTRICTIONS, EASEMENTS, LIMITATIONS: Buyer shall take title subject to: (a) Zoning, restrictions, prohibitions and requirements imposed by governmental authority, (b) Restrictions and matters appearing on the plat or common to the subdivision, (c) Public utility easements of record, provided said easements are located on the side or rear lines of the property, (d) Taxes for year of closing, assumed mortgages, and purchase money mortgages, if any, (e) Other: _____
_____. Seller warrants that there shall be no violations of building or zoning codes at the time of closing.

5. DEFAULT BY BUYER: If Buyer fails to perform any of the covenants of this contract, all money paid pursuant to this contract by Buyer as aforesaid shall be retained by or for the account of the Seller as consideration for the execution of this contract and as agreed liquidated damages and in full settlement of any claims for damages.

6. DEFAULT BY SELLER: If the Seller fails to perform any of the covenants of this contract, the aforesaid money paid by the Buyer, at the option of the Buyer, shall be returned to the Buyer on demand; or the Buyer shall have only the right of specific performance.

7. TERMITE INSPECTION: At least 15 days before closing, Buyer, at Buyer's expense, shall have the right to obtain a written report from a licensed exterminator stating that there is no evidence of live termite or other wood-boring insect infestation on said property nor substantial damage from prior infestation on said property. If there is such evidence, Seller shall pay up to three (3%) percent of the purchase price for the treatment required to remedy such infestation, including repairing and replacing portions of said improvements which have been damaged; but if the costs for such treatment or repairs exceed three (3%) percent of the purchase price, Buyer may elect to pay such excess. If Buyer elects not to pay, Seller may pay the excess or cancel the contract.

8. ROOF INSPECTION: At least 15 days before closing, Buyer, at Buyer's expense, shall have the right to obtain a written report from a licensed roofer stating that the roof is in a watertight condition. In the event repairs are required either to correct leaks or to replace damage to facia or soffit, Seller shall pay up to three (3%) percent of the purchase price for said repairs which shall be performed by a licensed roofing contractor; but if the costs for such repairs exceed three (3%) percent of the purchase price, Buyer may elect to pay such excess. If Buyer elects not to pay, Seller may pay the excess or cancel the contract.

9. OTHER INSPECTIONS: At least 15 days before closing, Buyer or his agent may inspect all appliances, air conditioning and heating systems, electrical systems, plumbing, machinery, sprinklers and pool system included in the sale. Seller shall pay for repairs necessary to place such items in working order at the time of closing. Within 48 hours before closing, Buyer shall be entitled, upon reasonable notice to Seller, to inspect the premises to determine that said items are in working order. All items of personal property included in the sale shall be transferred by Bill of Sale with warranty of title.

10. LEASES: Seller, not less than 15 days before closing, shall furnish to Buyer copies of all written leases and estoppel letters from each tenant specifying the nature and duration of the tenant's occupancy, rental rates and advanced rent and security deposits paid by tenant. If Seller is unable to obtain such letters from tenants, Seller shall furnish the same information to Buyer within said time period in the form of a seller's affidavit, and Buyer may contact tenants thereafter to confirm such information. At closing, seller shall deliver and assign all original leases to Buyer.

11. MECHANICS LIENS: Seller shall furnish to Buyer an affidavit that there have been no improvements to the subject property for 90 days immediately preceding the date of closing, and no financing statements, claims of lien or potential lienors known to Seller. If the property has been improved within that time, Seller shall deliver releases or waivers of all mechanics liens as executed by general contractors, subcontractors, suppliers and materialmen, in addition to the seller's lien affidavit, setting forth the names of all general contractors, subcontractors, suppliers and materialmen and reciting that all bills for work to the subject property which could serve as basis for mechanics liens have been paid or will be paid at closing.

12. PLACE OF CLOSING: Closing shall be held at the office of the Seller's attorney or as otherwise agreed upon.

13. TIME IS OF THE ESSENCE: Time is of the essence of this Sale and Purchase Agreement.

14. DOCUMENTS FOR CLOSING: Seller's attorney shall prepare deed, note, mortgage, Seller's affidavit, any corrective instruments required for perfecting the title, and closing statement and submit copies of same to Buyer's attorney, and copy of closing statement to the broker, at least two days prior to scheduled closing date.

15. EXPENSES: State documentary stamps required on the instrument of conveyance and the cost of recording any corrective instruments shall be paid by the Seller. Documentary stamps to be affixed to the note secured by the purchase money mortgage, intangible tax on the mortgage, and the cost of recording the deed and purchasing money mortgage shall be paid by the Buyer.

16. INSURANCE: If insurance is to be prorated, the Seller shall on or before the closing date, furnish to Buyer all insurance policies or copies thereof.

17. RISK OF LOSS: If the improvements are damaged by fire or casualty before delivery of the deed and can be restored to substantially the same condition as now within a period of 60 days thereafter, Seller shall so restore the improvements and the closing date and date of delivery of possession hereinbefore provided shall be extended accordingly. If Seller fails to do so, the Buyer shall have the option of (1) taking the property as is, together with insurance proceeds, if any, or (2) cancelling the contract, and all deposits shall be forthwith returned to the Buyer and all parties shall be released of any and all obligations and liability.

18. MAINTENANCE: Between the date of the contract and the date of closing, the property, including lawn, shrubbery and pool, if any, shall be maintained by the Seller in the condition as it existed as of the date of the contract, ordinary wear and tear excepted.

19. CLOSING DATE: This contract shall be closed and the deed and possession shall be delivered on or before the _____ day of _____ , _____ (year) , unless extended by other provisions of this contract.

20. TYPEWRITTEN OR HANDWRITTEN PROVISIONS: Typewritten or handwritten provisions inserted in this form shall control all printed provisions in conflict therewith.

21. OTHER AGREEMENTS: No agreements or representations, unless incorporated in this contract, shall be binding upon any of the parties.

22. RADON GAS DISCLOSURE: As required by law, (Landlord) (Seller) makes the following disclosure: "Radon Gas" is a naturally occurring radioactive gas that, when it has accumulated in a building in sufficient quantities, may present health risks to persons who are exposed to it over time. Levels of radon that exceed federal and state guidelines have been found in buildings in _____. Additional information regarding radon and radon testing may be obtained from your county public health unit.

23. LEAD PAINT DISCLOSURE: "Every purchaser of any interest in residential real property on which a residential dwelling was built prior to 1978 is notified that such property may present exposure to lead from lead-based paint that may place young children at risk of developing lead poisoning. Lead poisoning in young children may produce permanent neurological damage, including learning disabilities, reduced intelligence quotient, behavioral problems and impaired memory. Lead poisoning also poses a particular risk to pregnant women. The seller of any interest in residential real estate is required to provide the buyer with any information on lead-based paint hazards from risk assessments or inspection in the seller's possession and notify the buyer of any known lead-based paint hazards. A risk assessment or inspection for possible lead-based paint hazards is recommended prior to purchase."

24. SPECIAL CLAUSES:

COMMISSION TO BROKER: The Seller hereby recognizes _____
_____as the Broker in this transaction, and agrees to pay as commission
_____% of the gross sales price, the sum of _____
_____Dollars ($_____) or one-half of the deposit in case same is forfeited by the Buyer through failure to perform, as compensation for services rendered, provided same does not exceed the full amount of the commission.

WITNESSED BY:

_____   _____
Witness   Date   Buyer   Date

_____   _____
Witness   Date   Seller   Date

ASSIGNMENT OF MORTGAGE

BE IT KNOWN, that

party of the first part,

in consideration of the sum of

Dollars ($), and other valuable considerations, received from
or on behalf of

party of

the second part, the receipt whereof is hereby acknowledged, do hereby grant, bargain, sell, assign, transfer and set over unto the said party of the second part a certain mortgage dated the day of   ,   (year) made by

in favor of
and recorded in Official Records Book   , page   , public land records of
County, State of   , upon the following
described parcel of land, situate and being in said County and State, to wit:

Together with the note or obligation described in said mortgage, and the moneys due and to become due thereon, with interest from the   day of   ,   (year).

TO HAVE AND TO HOLD the same unto the said party of the second part, its heirs, legal representatives, successors and assigns forever.

IN WITNESS WHEREOF, I have hereunder set my hand and seal this   day of

                                    ,   (year).

Signed, sealed and delivered in presence of:

_____   _____
Witness   First Party

_____   _____
Witness   Second Party

State of
County of   }

On   before me,   ,
appeared
personally known to me (or proved to me on the basis of satisfactory evidence) to be the person(s) whose name(s) is/are subscribed to the within instrument and acknowledged to me that he/she/they executed the same in his/her/their authorized capacity(ies), and that by his/her/their signature(s) on the instrument the person(s), or the entity upon behalf of which the person(s) acted, executed the instrument.
WITNESS my hand and official seal.

Signature_____
                Signature of Notary   Affiant
                                                        _____Known_____Produced ID
                                                Type of ID_____
                                                                        (Seal)

_____
Signature of Preparer

_____
Print name of Preparer

_____
Address of Preparer

_____
City, State, Zip

BALLOON NOTE

FOR VALUE RECEIVED, the undersigned promise to pay to the order of

the sum of

Dollars ($), with annual interest of   % on any

unpaid balance.

This note shall be paid in   consecutive and equal installments of $

each with a first payment one   from date hereof, and the same amount on the same

day of each   thereafter, provided the entire principal balance and any accrued

but unpaid interest shall be fully paid on or before   ,   (year). This note

may be prepaid without penalty. All payments shall be first applied to interest and the balance to

principal.

This note shall be due and payable upon demand of any holder hereof should the under-

signed default in any payment beyond   days of its due date. All parties to this note

waive presentment, demand and protest, and all notices thereto. In the event of default, the under-

signed agree to pay all costs of collection and reasonable attorneys' fees. The undersigned shall

be jointly and severally liable under this note.

Signed this   day of   ,   (year).

Signed in the presence of:

_____   _____
Witness   Maker

_____   _____
Witness   Maker

COUNTER OFFER

In response to purchase and sales agreement executed and dated _____

between _____ (Buyers)

and _____ (Sellers),

for the sale of real property known as _____

_____,

Sellers make the following counter offer:

All other terms remain the same. The above counter offer, unless accepted, shall expire at _____ o'clock _____.m. on _____. A signed and properly executed copy returned to the Sellers prior to the deadline shall constitute acceptance of this offer.

Sellers shall retain the right to accept any offer tendered prior to acceptance of this counter offer.

_____   _____
Seller   Date

_____   _____
Seller   Date

_____   _____
Buyer   Date

_____   _____
Buyer   Date

DISCHARGE OF MORTGAGE

BE IT KNOWN, that for value received, we _____ ,

of _____ holders of a certain real

estate mortgage from _____ to _____ ,

said mortgage dated _____ , _____ (year), and recorded in Book or Volume _____ , Page

_____ , of the _____ County Registry of Deeds, acknowledge full satisfaction

and discharge of same.

Signed under seal this _____ day of _____ , _____ (year).

_____

_____

STATE OF _____ }
COUNTY OF _____

On _____ before me, _____ , personally appeared

_____ , personally known to me (or

proved to me on the basis of satisfactory evidence) to be the person(s) whose name(s) is/are subscribed to the within instrument and acknowledged to me that he/she/they executed the same in
his/her/their authorized capacity(ies), and that by his/her/their signature(s) on the instrument the
person(s), or the entity upon behalf of which the person(s) acted, executed the instrument.
WITNESS my hand and official seal.

Signature_____   Affiant _____Known _____Unknown
                                            ID Produced_____
                                                                    (Seal)

_____   _____
Signature of Preparer   Address of Preparer

_____   _____
Print name of Preparer   City, State, Zip

ESCROW AGREEMENT

AGREEMENT between   , (Seller)
, (Buyer) and
, (Escrow Agent).

Simultaneously with the making of this Agreement, Seller and Buyer have entered into a contract (the Contract) by which Seller will sell to Buyer the following property:

The closing will take place on   ,   (year), at   .m., at the offices of   , located at   , or at such other time and place as Seller and Buyer may jointly designate in writing. Pursuant to the Contract, Buyer must deposit $ as a down payment to be held in escrow by Escrow Agent.

The $ down payment referred to hereinabove has been paid by Buyer to Escrow Agent. Escrow Agent acknowledges receipt of $ from Buyer by check, subject to collection.

If the closing takes place under the Contract, Escrow Agent at the time of closing shall pay the amount deposited with Agent to Seller or in accordance with Seller's written instructions. Escrow Agent shall make simultaneous transfer of the said property to the Buyer.

If no closing takes place under the Contract, Escrow Agent shall continue to hold the amount deposited until receipt of written authorization for its disposition signed by both Buyer and Seller. If there is any dispute as to whom Escrow Agent is to deliver the amount deposited, Escrow Agent shall hold the sum until the parties' rights are finally determined in an appropriate action or proceeding or until a court orders Escrow Agent to deposit the down payment with it. If Escrow Agent does not receive a proper written authorization from Seller and Buyer, or if an action or proceeding to determine Seller's and Buyer's rights is not begun or diligently prosecuted, Escrow Agent is under no obligation to bring an action or proceeding in court to deposit the sum held, but may continue to hold the deposit.

Escrow Agent assumes no liability except that of a stakeholder. Escrow Agent's duties are limited to those specifically set out in this Agreement. Escrow Agent shall incur no liability to anyone except for willful misconduct or gross negligence so long as the Escrow Agent acts in good faith. Seller and Buyer release Escrow Agent from any act done or omitted in good faith in the performance of Escrow Agent's duties.

Special provisions:

Whereof the parties sign their names this   day of   ,   (year).

Signed in the presence of:

_____   _____
Witness   Seller

_____   _____
Witness   Buyer

_____   _____
Witness   Escrow Agent

EXCLUSIVE RIGHT TO SELL

For and in consideration of your services to be rendered in listing for sale and in undertaking to sell or find a purchaser for the property hereinafter described, the parties understand and agree that this is an exclusive listing to sell the real estate located at:

,

together with the following improvements and fixtures:

The minimum selling price of the property shall be

dollars ($), to be payable on the following terms:

You are authorized to accept and hold a deposit in the amount of

dollars ($) as a deposit and to apply such deposit on the purchase price.

If said property is sold, traded or in any other way disposed of either by us or by anyone else within the time specified in this listing, it is agreed to and understood that you shall receive from the sale or trade of said property as your commission   percent (%) of the purchase price. Should said property be sold or traded within   days after expiration of this listing agreement to a purchaser with whom you have been negotiating for the sale or trade of the property, the said commission shall be due and payable on demand.

We agree to furnish a certificate of title showing a good and merchantable title of record, and further agree to convey by good and sufficient warranty deed or guaranteed title on payment in full.

This listing contract shall continue until midnight of _____ , _____ (year).

Date:

_____
Owner

_____
Owner

I accept this listing and agree to act promptly and diligently to procure a buyer for said property.

Date:

_____

EXERCISE OF OPTION

Date:

To:

     You are hereby notified that the undersigned has elected to and does hereby exercise and accept the option dated _____ , _____ (year), executed by you as seller to the under-signed as purchaser, and agrees to all terms, conditions, and provisions of the option.

                                      _____

GENERAL LEAD DISCLOSURE INFORMATION

(1) Lead-based paint hazards

The regulations effective October 28, 1995 shall require that, before the purchaser or lessee is obligated under any contract to purchase or lease the housing, the seller or lessor shall—

(A) provide the purchaser or lessee with a lead hazard information pamphlet, as prescribed by the Administrator of the Environmental Protection Agency under section 406 of the Toxic Substances Control Act [15 U.S.C.A. s 2686];

(B) disclose to the purchaser or lessee the presence of any known lead-based paint, or any known lead-based paint hazards, in such housing and provide to the purchaser or lessee any lead hazard evaluation report available to the seller or lessor; and

(C) permit the purchaser a 10-day period (unless the parties mutually agree upon a different period of time) to conduct a risk assessment or inspection for the presence of lead-based paint hazards.

(2) Contract for purchase and sale

Regulations promulgated under this section shall provide that every contract for the purchase and sale of any interest in target housing shall contain a Lead Warning Statement and a statement signed by the purchaser that the purchaser has—

(A) read the Lead Warning Statement and understands its contents;

(B) received a lead hazard information pamphlet; and

(C) had a 10-day opportunity (unless the parties mutually agreed upon a different period of time) before becoming obligated under the contract to purchase the housing to conduct a risk assessment or inspection for the presence of lead-based paint hazards.

(3) Compliance assurance

Whenever a seller or lessor has entered into a contract with an agent for the purpose of selling or leasing a unit of target housing, the regulations promulgated under this section shall require the agent, on behalf of the seller or lessor, to ensure compliance with the requirements of this section.

(4) Penalties for violations

Penalties shall include monetary penalties, action by the Secretary of State, civil liability equal to three times the amount of damages, costs and attorney and expert witness fees.

(5) Validity of contracts and liens

Nothing in this section shall affect the validity or enforceability of any sale or contract for the purchase and sale or lease of any interest in residential real property or any loan, loan agreement, mortgage, or lien made or arising in connection with a mortgage loan, nor shall anything in this section create a defect in title.

LEAD DISCLOSURE STATEMENT
FOR SALE OF RESIDENTIAL PROPERTY

LEAD WARNING STATEMENT: Every purchaser of any interest in residential real property on which a residential dwelling was built prior to 1978 is notified that such property may present exposure to lead from lead-based paint that may place young children at risk of developing lead poisoning. Lead poisoning in young children may produce permanent neurological damage, including learning disabilities, reduced intelligence quotient, behavioral problems, and impaired memory. Lead poisoning also poses a particular risk to pregnant women. The seller of any interest in residential real property is required to provide the buyer with any information on lead-based paint hazards from risk assessments or inspections in the seller's possession and notify the buyer of any known lead-based paint hazards. A risk assessment or inspection for possible lead-based paint hazards is recommended prior to purchase.

SELLER'S DISCLOSURE (initial)

(a) Presence of lead-based paint and/or lead-based paint.

    (i) _____ Known lead-based paint and/or lead-based paint hazards are present in the housing (explain).

    (ii) _____ Seller has no knowledge of lead-based paint and/or lead-based paint hazards in the housing.

(b) Records and reports available to the seller (check (i) or (ii) below):

    (i) _____ Seller has provided the purchaser with all available records and reports pertaining to lead-based paint and/or lead-based paint hazards in the housing (list documents below).

    (ii) _____ Seller has no reports or records pertaining to lead-based paint and/or lead-based paint hazards in the housing.

PURCHASER'S ACKNOWLEDGMENT (initial)

(c) _____ Purchaser has received copies of all information listed above.

(d) _____ Purchaser has received the pamphlet "Protect Your Family from Lead in Your Home."

(e) Purchaser has (check (i) or (ii) below):

    (i) _____ received a 10-day opportunity (or mutually agreed upon period) to conduct a risk assessment or inspection for the presence of lead-based paint and/or lead-based paint hazards; or

    (ii) _____ waived the opportunity to conduct a risk assessment or inspection for the presence of lead-based paint and/or lead-based paint hazards.

AGENT'S ACKNOWLEDGMENT (initial)

(f) _____ Agent has informed the seller of the seller's obligations under 42 U.S.C. 4852d and is aware of his/her responsibility to ensure compliance.

CERTIFICATION OF ACCURACY

The following parties have reviewed the information above and certify, to the best of their knowledge, that the information they have provided is true and accurate.

Seller	Date	Seller	Date
Purchaser	Date	Purchaser	Date
Agent	Date	Agent	Date

Protect Your Family From Lead in Your Home

United States Environmental Protection Agency
United States Consumer Product Safety Commission

Are You Planning To Buy, Rent, or Renovate a Home Built Before 1978?

Many houses and apartments built before 1978 have paint that contains lead (called lead-based paint). Lead from paint, chips, and dust can pose serious health hazards if not taken care of properly.

By 1996, federal law will require that individuals receive certain information before renting, buying, or renovating pre-1978 housing:

LANDLORDS will have to disclose known information on lead-based paint hazards before leases take effect. Leases will include a federal form about lead-based paint.

SELLERS will have to disclose known information on lead-based paint hazards before selling a house. Sales contracts will include a federal form about lead-based paint in the building. Buyers will have up to 10 days to check for lead hazards.

RENOVATORS will have to give you this pamphlet before starting work.

IF YOU WANT MORE INFORMATION on these requirements, call the National Lead Information Clearinghouse at 1-800-424-LEAD.

IMPORTANT! Lead From Paint, Dust, and Soil Can Be Dangerous If Not Managed Properly

FACT: Lead exposure can harm young children and babies even before they are born.

FACT: Even children that seem healthy can have high levels of lead in their bodies.

FACT: People can get lead in their bodies by breathing or swallowing lead dust, or by eating soil or paint chips with lead in them.

FACT: People have many options for reducing lead hazards. In most cases, lead-based paint that is in good condition is not a hazard.

FACT: Removing lead-based paint improperly can increase the danger to your family.

If you think your home might have lead hazards, read this pamphlet to learn some simple steps to protect your family.

Lead Gets in the Body in Many Ways

People can get lead in their body if they:

* Put their hands or other objects covered with lead dust in their mouths.
* Eat paint chips or soil that contains lead.
* Breathe in lead dust (especially during renovations that disturb painted surfaces).

Lead is even more dangerous to children than adults because:

* Babies and young children often put their hands and other objects in their mouths. These objects can have lead dust on them.
* Children's growing bodies absorb more lead.
* Children's brains and nervous systems are more sensitive to the damaging effects of lead.

1 out of every 11 children in the United States has dangerous levels of lead in the bloodstream.

Even children who appear healthy can have dangerous levels of lead.

Lead's Effects

If not detected early, children with high levels of lead in their bodies can suffer from:

* Damage to the brain and nervous system
* Behavior and learning problems (such as hyperactivity)
* Slowed growth
* Hearing problems
* Headaches

Lead is also harmful to adults. Adults can suffer from:

* Difficulties during pregnancy
* Other reproductive problems (in both men and women)
* High blood pressure
* Digestive problems
* Nerve disorders
* Memory and concentration problems
* Muscle and joint pain

Checking Your Family for Lead

Get your children tested if you think your home has high levels of lead

A simple blood test can detect high levels of lead. Blood tests are important for:

* Children who are 6 months to 1 year old (6 months if you live in an older home with cracking or peeling paint).
* Family members you think might have high levels of lead.

If your child is older than 1 year, talk to your doctor about whether your child needs testing.

Your doctor or health center can do blood tests. They are inexpensive and sometimes free. Your doctor will explain what the test results mean. Treatment can range from changes in your diet to medication or a hospital stay.

Where Lead-Based Paint Is Found

In general, the older your home, the more likely it has lead-based paint.

Many homes built before 1978 have lead-based paint. The federal government banned lead-based paint from housing in 1978. Some states stopped its use even earlier. Lead can be found:

* In homes in the city, country, or suburbs.
* In apartments, single-family homes, and both private and public housing.
* Inside and outside of the house.
* In soil around a home. (Soil can pick up lead from exterior paint, or other sources such as past use of leaded gas in cars.)

Where Lead Is Likely To Be a Hazard

Lead from paint chips, which you can see, and lead dust, which you can't always see, can both be serious hazards.

Lead-based paint in good condition is usually not a hazard.

Peeling, chipping, chalking, or cracking lead-based paint is a hazard and needs immediate attention.

Lead-based paint may also be a hazard when found on surfaces that children can chew or that get a lot of wear-and-tear. These areas include:

* Windows and window sills.
* Doors and door frames.
* Stairs, railings, and banisters.
* Porches and fences.

Lead dust can form when lead-based paint is dry scraped, dry sanded, or heated. Dust also forms when painted surfaces bump or rub together. Lead chips and dust can get on surfaces and objects that people touch. Settled lead dust can reenter the air when people vacuum, sweep, or walk through it.

Lead in soil can be a hazard when children play in bare soil or when people bring soil into the house on their shoes. Call your state agency to find out about soil testing for lead.

Checking Your Home for Lead Hazards

Just knowing that a home has lead-based paint may not tell you if there is a hazard.

You can get your home checked for lead hazards in one of two ways, or both:

• A paint inspection tells you the lead content of every painted surface in your home. It won't tell you whether the paint is a hazard or how you should deal with it.

• A risk assessment tells you if there are any sources of serious lead exposure (such as peeling paint and lead dust). It also tells you what actions to take to address these hazards.

Have qualified professionals do the work. The federal government is writing standards for inspectors and risk assessors. Some states might already have standards in place. Call your state agency for help with locating qualified professionals in your area.

Trained professionals use a range of methods when checking your home, including:

• Visual inspection of paint condition and location.
• Lab tests of paint samples.
• Surface dust tests.
• A portable x-ray fluorescence machine.

Home test kits for lead are available, but recent studies suggest that they are not always accurate. Consumers should not rely on these tests before doing renovations or to assure safety.

What You Can Do Now To Protect Your Family

If you suspect that your house has lead hazards, you can take some immediate steps to reduce your family's risk:

• If you rent, notify your landlord of peeling or chipping paint.
• Clean up paint chips immediately.
• Clean floors, window frames, window sills, and other surfaces weekly. Use a mop or sponge with warm water and a general all-purpose cleaner or a cleaner made specifically for lead. REMEMBER: NEVER MIX AMMONIA AND BLEACH PRODUCTS TOGETHER SINCE THEY CAN FORM A DANGEROUS GAS.
• Thoroughly rinse sponges and mop heads after cleaning dirty or dusty areas.
• Wash children's hands often, especially before they eat and before nap time and bed time.
• Keep play areas clean. Wash bottles, pacifiers, toys, and stuffed animals regularly.
• Keep children from chewing window sills or other painted surfaces.
• Clean or remove shoes before entering your home to avoid tracking in lead from soil.
• Make sure children eat nutritious, low-fat meals high in iron and calcium, such as spinach and low-fat dairy products. Children with good diets absorb less lead.

How To Significantly Reduce Lead Hazards

Removing lead improperly can increase the hazard to your family by spreading even more lead dust around the house.

Always use a professional who is trained to remove lead hazards safely.

In addition to day-to-day cleaning and good nutrition:

• You can temporarily reduce lead hazards by taking actions such as repairing damaged painted surfaces and planting grass to cover soil with high lead levels. These actions (called "interim controls") are not permanent solutions and will need ongoing attention.

• To permanently remove lead hazards, you must hire a lead "abatement" contractor. Abatement (or permanent hazard elimination) methods include removing, sealing, or enclosing lead-based paint with special materials. Just painting over the hazard with regular paint is not enough.

Always hire a person with special training for correcting lead problems—someone who knows how to do this work safely and has the proper equipment to clean up thoroughly. If possible, hire a certified lead abatement contractor. Certified contractors will employ qualified workers and follow strict safety rules as set by their state or by the federal government.

Call your state agency for help with locating qualified contractors in your area and to see if financial assistance is available.

Remodeling or Renovating a Home With Lead-Based Paint

If not conducted properly, certain types of renovations can release lead from paint and dust into the air.

Take precautions before you begin remodeling or renovations that disturb painted surfaces (such as scraping off paint or tearing out walls):

• Have the area tested for lead-based paint.
• Do not use a dry scraper, belt-sander, propane torch, or heat gun to remove lead-based paint. These actions create large amounts of lead dust and fumes. Lead dust can remain in your home long after the work is done.
• Temporarily move your family (especially children and pregnant women) out of the apartment or house until the work is done and the area is properly cleaned. If you can't move your family, at least completely seal off the work area.
• Follow other safety measures to reduce lead hazards. You can find out about other safety measures by calling 1-800-424-LEAD. Ask for the brochure "Reducing Lead Hazards When Remodeling Your Home." This brochure explains what to do before, during, and after renovations.
• Don't use a belt-sander, propane torch, dry scraper, or dry sandpaper on painted surfaces that may contain lead.
• Don't try to remove lead-based paint yourself.

If you have already completed renovations or remodeling that could have released lead-based paint or dust, get your young children tested and follow the steps outlined on this page.

Other Sources of Lead

While paint, dust, and soil are the most common lead hazards, other lead sources also exist.

• Drinking water. Your home might have plumbing with lead or lead solder. Call your local health department or water supplier to find out about testing your water. You cannot see, smell, or taste lead, and boiling your water will not get rid of lead. If you think your plumbing might have lead in it::
• Use only cold water for drinking and cooking.
• Run water for 15 to 30 seconds before drinking it,

especially if you have not used your water for a few hours.
- The job. If you work with lead, you could bring it home on your hands or clothes. Shower and change clothes before coming home. Launder your clothes separately from the rest of your family's.
- Old painted toys and furniture.
- Food and liquids stored in lead crystal or lead-glazed pottery or porcelain.
- Lead smelters or other industries that release lead into the air.
- Hobbies that use lead, such as making pottery or stained glass, or refinishing furniture.
- Folk remedies that contain lead, such as "greta" and "azarcon" used to treat an upset stomach.

Simple Steps To Protect Your Family From Lead Hazards
If you think your home has high levels of lead:
- Get your young children tested for lead, even if they seem healthy.
- Wash children's hands, bottles, pacifiers, and toys often.
- Make sure children eat healthy, low-fat foods.
- Get your home checked for lead hazards.
- Regularly clean floors, window sills, and other surfaces.
- Wipe soil off shoes before entering house.
- Talk to your landlord about fixing surfaces with peeling or chipping paint.
- Take precautions to avoid exposure to lead dust when remodeling or renovating (call 1-800-424-LEAD for guidelines).

For More Information

National Lead Information Center
Call 1-800-LEAD-FYI to learn how to protect children from lead poisoning. For other information on lead hazards, call the Center's Clearinghouse at 1-800-424-LEAD. For the hearing impaired, call, TDD 1-800-526-5456 (FAX: 202-659-1192, Internet: EHC@CAIS.COM).

EPA's Safe Drinking Water Hotline
Call 1-800-426-4791 for information about lead in drinking water.

Consumer Product Safety Commission Hotline
To request information on lead in consumer products, or to report an unsafe consumer product or a product-related injury call 1-800-638-2772. (Internet: info@cpsc.gov). For the hearing impaired, call TDD 1-800-638-8270.

State Health and Environmental Agencies
Some cities and states have their own rules for lead-based paint activities. Check with your state agency (listed below) to see if state or local laws apply to you. Most state agencies can also provide more information on finding a lead abatement firm in your area, and on possible sources of financial aid for reducing lead hazards.

State	Phone	State	Phone
Alabama	(205) 242-5661	Oregon	(503) 248-5240
Alaska	(907) 465-5152	Pennsylvania	(717) 782-2884
Arkansas	(501) 661-2534	Rhode Island	(401) 277-3424
Arizona	(602) 542-7307	South Carolina	(803) 935-7945
California	(510) 450-2424	South Dakota	(605) 773-3153
Colorado	(303) 692-3012	Tennessee	(615) 741-5683
Connecticut	(203) 566-5808	Texas	(512) 834-6600
Washington, D.C	(202) 727-9850	Utah	(801) 536-4000
Delaware	(302) 739-4735	Vermont	(802) 863-7231
Florida	(904) 488-3385	Virginia	(800) 523-4019
Georgia	(404) 657-6514	Washington	(206) 753-2556
Hawaii	(808) 832-5860	West Virginia	(304) 558-2981
Idaho	(208) 332-5544	Wisconsin	(608) 266-5885
Illinois	(800) 545-2200	Wyoming	(307) 777-7391
Indiana	(317) 382-6662		
Iowa	(800) 972-2026		
Kansas	(913) 296-0189		
Kentucky	(502) 564-2154		
Louisiana	(504) 765-0219		
Massachusetts	(800) 532-9571		
Maryland	(410) 631-3859		
Maine	(207) 287-4311		
Michigan	(517) 335-8885		
Minnesota	(612) 627-5498		
Mississippi	(601) 960-7463		
Missouri	(314) 526-4911		
Montana	(406) 444-3671		
Nebraska	(402) 471-2451		
Nevada	(702) 687-6615		
New Hampshire	(603) 271-4507		
New Jersey	(609) 633-2043		
New Mexico	(505) 841-8024		
New York	(800) 458-1158		
North Carolina	(919) 715-3293		
North Dakota	(701) 328-5188		
Ohio	(614) 466-1450		
Oklahoma	(405) 271-5220		

EPA Regional Offices
Your Regional EPA Office can provide further information regarding regulations and lead protection programs.

Region 1 (Connecticut, Massachusetts, Maine, New Hampshire, Rhode Island, Vermont)
JFK Federal Building
One Congress Street
Boston, MA 02203
(617) 565-3420

Region 2
(New Jersey, New York, Puerto Rico, Virgin Islands)
Building 5
2890 Woodbridge Avenue
Edison, NJ 08837-3679
(908) 321-6671

Region 3
(Delaware, Washington DC, Maryland, Pennsylvania, Virginia, West Virginia)
841 Chestnut Building
Philadelphia, PA 19107
(215) 597-9800

Region 4
(Alabama, Florida, Georgia, Kentucky, Mississippi, North Carolina, South Carolina, Tennessee)
345 Courtland Street, NE
Atlanta, GA 30365
(404) 347-4727

Region 5
(Illinois, Indiana, Michigan, Minnesota, Ohio, Wisconsin)
77 West Jackson Boulevard
Chicago, IL 60604-3590
(312) 886-6003

Region 6
(Arkansas, Louisiana, New Mexico, Oklahoma, Texas)
First Interstate Bank Tower
1445 Ross Avenue, 12th Floor
Suite 1200
Dallas, TX 75202-2733
(214) 665-7244

Region 7
(Iowa, Kansas, Missouri, Nebraska)
726 Minnesota Avenue
Kansas City, KS 66101
(913) 551-7020

Region 8
(Colorado, Montana, N.Dakota, S. Dakota, Utah, Wyoming)
999 18th Street, Suite 500
Denver, CO 80202-2405
(303) 293-1603

Region 9
(Arizona, California, Hawaii, Nevada)
75 Hawthorne Street
San Francisco, CA 94105
(415) 744-1124

Region 10
(Idaho, Oregon, Wash., Alaska)
1200 Sixth Avenue
Seattle, WA 98101
(206) 553-1200

EPA/CPSC Regional Offices

Eastern Regional Center
6 World Trade Center
Vesey Street, Room 350
New York, NY 10048
(212) 466-1612

Central Regional Center
230 South Dearborn Street
Room 2944
Chicago, IL 60604-1601
(312) 353-8260

Western Regional Center
600 Harrison Street, Room 245
San Francisco, CA 94107
(415) 744-2966

LEASE WITH PURCHASE OPTION

BY THIS AGREEMENT made and entered into on   ,   (year), between   ,
herein referred to as Lessor, and   ,
herein referred to as Lessee, Lessor leases to Lessee the premises situated at
                                    , in the City of   , County of
            , State of   , and more particularly described as follows:
                                                                                                                                          ,
together with all appurtenances, for a term of   years, to commence on
                    ,   (year), and to end on   ,   (year), at o'clock   . m.

1. Rent. Lessee agrees to pay, without demand, to Lessor as rent for the demised premises the sum of
                    Dollars ($)   per
month in advance on the   day of each calendar month beginning   ,   (year),
payable at
City of   , State of   , or at such other place as Lessor may designate.

2. Security Deposit. On execution of this lease, Lessee deposits with Lessor
                    Dollars ($), receipt of which is acknowledged by Lessor, as security for
the faithful performance by Lessee of the terms hereof, to be returned to Lessee, without interest, on the full and
faithful performance by him of the provisions hereof.

3. Quiet Enjoyment. Lessor covenants that on paying the rent and performing the covenants there in contained,
Lessee shall peacefully and quietly have, hold, and enjoy the demised premises for the agreed term.

4. Use of Premises. The demised premises shall be used and occupied by Lessee exclusively as
                                    , and neither the premises nor any part thereof shall be used at any time during
the term of this lease by Lessee for any other purpose. Lessee shall comply with all the sanitary laws, ordinances,
rules, and orders of appropriate governmental authorities affecting the cleanliness, occupancy, and preservation of
the demised premises, and the sidewalks connected thereto, during the term of this lease.

5. Condition of Premises. Lessee stipulates that he has examined the demised premises, including the grounds and
all buildings and improvements, and that they are, at the time of this lease, in good order, repair, and in a safe, clean,
and tenantable condition.

6. Assignment and Subletting. Without the prior written consent of Lessor, Lessee shall not assign this lease, or sub-
let or grant any concession or license to use the premises or any part thereof. A consent by Lessor to one assignment,
subletting, concession, or license shall not be deemed to be a consent to any subsequent assignment, subletting, concession, or license. An assignment, subletting, concession, or license without the prior written consent of Lessor, or an
assignment or subletting by operation of law, shall be void and shall, at Lessor's option, terminate this lease.

7. Alterations and Improvements. Lessee shall make no alterations to the buildings or the demised premises or
construct any building or make other improvements on the demised premises without the prior written consent of
Lessor. All alterations, changes, and improvements built, constructed, or placed on the demised premises by Lessee,
with the exception of fixtures removable without damage to the premises and movable personal property, shall,
unless otherwise provided by written agreement between Lessor and Lessee, be the property of Lessor and remain
on the demised premises at the expiration or upon sooner termination of this lease.

8. Damage to Premises. If the demised premises, or any part thereof, shall be partially damaged by fire or other casualty not due to Lessee's negligence or willful act or that of his employee, family, agent, or visitor, the premises shall be promptly repaired by Lessor and there shall be an abatement of rent corresponding with the time during which, and the extent to which, the leased premises may have been untenantable; but, if the leased premises should be damaged other than by Lessee's negligence or willful act or that of his employee, family, agent, or visitor to the extent that Lessor shall decide not to rebuild or repair, the term of this lease shall end and the rent shall be prorated up to the time of the damage.

9. Dangerous Materials. Lessee shall not keep or have on the leased premises anything of a dangerous, inflammable, or explosive character that might unreasonably increase the danger of fire on the leased premises or that might be considered hazardous or extra hazardous by any responsible insurance company.

10. Utilities. Lessee shall be responsible for arranging for and paying for all utility services required on the premises, except that   shall be provided by Lessor.

11. Maintenance and Repair. Lessee will, at his sole expense, keep and maintain the leased premises and appurtenances in good and sanitary condition and repair during the term of this lease and any renewal thereof. In particular, Lessee shall keep the fixtures on or about the leased premises in good order and repair; keep the furnace clean; keep the electric bells in order; keep the walks free from dirt and debris; and, at his sole expense, shall make all required repairs to the plumbing, range, heating apparatus, and electric and gas fixtures whenever damage thereto shall have resulted from Lessee's misuse, waste, or neglect or that of his employee, family, agent, or visitor. Major maintenance and repair of the leased premises, not due to Lessee's misuse, waste, or neglect or that of his employee, family, agent, or visitor, shall be the responsibility of Lessor or his assigns. Lessee agrees that no signs shall be placed or painting done on or about the leased premises by Lessee or at his direction without the prior written consent of Lessor.

12. Right of Inspection. Lessor and his agents shall have the right at all reasonable times during the term of this lease and any renewal thereof to enter the demised premises for the purpose of inspecting the premises and all building and improvements thereon.

13. Display of Signs. During the last   days of this lease, Lessor or his agent shall have the privilege of displaying the usual "For Sale" or "For Rent" or "Vacancy" signs on the demised premises and of showing the property to prospective purchasers or tenants.

14. Subordination of Lease. This lease and Lessee's leasehold interest hereunder are and shall be subject, subordinate, and inferior to, any liens or encumbrances now or hereafter placed on the demised premises by Lessor, all advances made under any such liens or encumbrances, the interest payable on any such liens or encumbrances, and any and all renewals or extensions of such liens or encumbrances.

15. Holdover by Lessee. Should Lessee remain in possession of the demised premises with the consent of Lessor after the natural expiration of this lease, a new month-to-month tenancy shall be created between Lessor and Lessee which shall be subject to all the terms and conditions hereof but shall be terminated on   days' written notice served by either Lessor or Lessee on the other party.

16. Surrender of Premises. At the expiration of the lease term, Lessee shall quit and surrender the premises hereby demised in as good state and condition as they were at the commencement of this lease, reasonable use and wear thereof and damages by the elements excepted.

17. Default. If any default is made in the payment of rent, or any part thereof, at the times hereinbefore specified, or if any default is made in the performance of or compliance with any other term or condition hereof, this lease, at the option of Lessor, shall terminate and be forfeited, and Lessor may re-enter the premises and remove all persons therefrom. Lessee shall be given written notice of any default or breach, and termination and forfeiture of the lease shall not result if, within   days of receipt of such notice, Lessee has corrected the default or breach or has taken action reasonably likely to effect such correction within a reasonable time. Lessee shall pay all reasonable attorneys' fees necessary to enforce lessor's rights.

18. Abandonment. If at any time during the term of this lease Lessee abandons the demised premises or any part thereof, Lessor may, at his option, enter the demised premises by any means without being liable for any prosecution therefore, and without becoming liable to Lessee for damages or for any payment of any kind whatever, and may, at his discretion, as agent for Lessee, relet the demised premises, or any part thereof, for the whole or any part of the then unexpired term, and may receive and collect all rent payable by virtue of such reletting, and, at Lessor's option, hold Lessee liable for any difference between the rent that would have been payable under this lease during the balance of the unexpired term, if this lease had continued in force, and the net rent for such period realized by Lessor by means of such reletting. If Lessor's right of re-entry is exercised following abandonment of the premises by Lessee, then Lessor may consider any personal property belonging to Lessee and left on the premises to also have been abandoned, in which case Lessor may dispose of all such personal property in any manner Lessor shall deem proper and is hereby relieved of all liability for doing so.

19. Binding Effect. The covenants and conditions herein contained shall apply to and bind the heirs, legal representatives, and assigns of the parties hereto, and all covenants are to be construed as conditions of this lease.

20. Purchase Option. It is agreed that Lessee shall have the option to purchase real estate known as:

for the purchase price of   Dollars ($) with a down payment of   Dollars ($) payable upon exercise of said purchase option, and with a closing date no later than   days thereafter. This purchase option must be exercised in writing no later than   ,   (year), but shall not be effective should the Lessee be in default under any terms of this lease or upon any termination of this lease.

21. Radon Gas Disclosure. As required by law, (Landlord) (Seller) makes the following disclosure: "Radon Gas" is a naturally occurring radioactive gas that, when it has accumulated in a building in sufficient quantities, may present health risks to persons who are exposed to it over time. Levels of radon that exceed federal and state guidelines have been found in buildings in   . Additional information regarding radon and radon testing may be obtained from your county public health unit.

22. Lead Paint Disclosure. "Every purchaser of any interest in residential real property on which a residential dwelling was built prior to 1978 is notified that such property may present exposure to lead from lead-based paint that may place young children at risk of developing lead poisoning. Lead poisoning in young children may produce permanent neurological damage, including learning disabilities, reduced intelligence quotient, behavioral problems and impaired memory. Lead poisoning also poses a particular risk to pregnant women. The seller of any interest in residential real estate is required to provide the buyer with any information on lead-based paint hazards from risk assessments or inspection in the seller's possession and notify the buyer of any known lead-based paint hazards. A risk assessment or inspection for possible lead-based paint hazards is recommended prior to purchase."

23. Other Options.

IN WITNESS WHEREOF, the parties have executed this lease on the day and year first above written.

_____
Lessor

_____
Lessee

_____
Signature of Preparer

_____
Address of Preparer

_____
Print name of Preparer

_____
City, State, Zip

NOTICE: State law establishes rights and obligations for parties to rental agreements. This agreement is required to comply with the Truth in Renting Act or the applicable Landlord Tenant Statute or code of your state. If you have a question about the interpretation or legality of a provision of this agreement, you may want to seek assistance from a lawyer or other qualified person.

Contact your local county real estate board or Association of Realtors® for additional forms that may be required to meet your specific needs.

MONTHLY BUDGET PLANNER

	Husband	**Wife**	
Average Salary	_____	_____	
Average Commission	_____	_____	
Benefits	_____	_____	
Investment dividends	_____	_____	
Retirement Plans/Profit Sharing	_____	_____	
Other ( )	_____	_____	
TOTAL MONTHLY INCOME	_____	_____	_____

	Present	**Proposed**	
Rent/Mortgage Payment	_____	_____	
Electricity	_____	_____	
Water	_____	_____	
Phone	_____	_____	
Cable	_____	_____	
Trash pickup	_____	_____	
Lawn service	_____	_____	
Property tax	_____	_____	
Homeowners insurance	_____	_____	
Auto payments	_____	_____	
Auto maintenance	_____	_____	
Auto insurance	_____	_____	
Food	_____	_____	
Clothing	_____	_____	
Child care	_____	_____	
Education	_____	_____	
Child support	_____	_____	
Alimony	_____	_____	
Entertainment/Vacation	_____	_____	
Pet expenses	_____	_____	
Life/Health Insurance	_____	_____	
Medical/Dental/Optical expenses	_____	_____	
Credit cards	_____	_____	
Loans	_____	_____	
Other ( )	_____	_____	
Other ( )	_____	_____	
TOTAL MONTHLY SPENDING	_____	_____	_____

MORTGAGE BOND

KNOW ALL BY THESE PRESENTS, that
(Obligor) does hereby acknowledge that Obligor is indebted to   ,
having an office at
County of   , State of   (Obligee), in the principal
sum of
dollars ($), which sum with interest on the unpaid balances to be computed from the
date hereof at the rate of   percent (%) per annum, Obligor does covenant to pay
to Obligee, at the office of Obligee in   ,   or
such other place as Obligee may designate in writing,   dollars ($) on
the first day of   ,   (year), and thereafter in   payments of
          dollars ($) on the first day of each subsequent month, until the
principal and interest are fully paid, except that the final payment of the entire indebtedness
evidenced hereby, shall be due and payable on the first of   ,   (year).

The whole or any part of the principal sum and of any other sums of money secured by
the mortgage given to secure this Bond shall, at the option of Obligee, become due and payable
if default be made in any payment under this Bond or upon the happening of any default that, by
the terms of the mortgage given to secure this Bond, shall entitle the mortgagee to declare the
principal sum, or any part thereof, to be due and payable; and all the covenants, agreements,
terms, and conditions of the mortgage are incorporated in this Bond with the same force and effect
as if set forth at length.

If more than one person joins in the execution of this Bond, the relative words herein shall be read as if written in the plural, and the words "Obligor" and "Obligee" shall include their heirs, executors, administrators, successors and assigns.

Signed this _____ day of _____ , _____ (year).

_____
                                                    Obligor

STATE OF
COUNTY OF   }

On _____ before me, _____ , personally appeared _____ , personally known to me (or proved to me on the basis of satisfactory evidence) to be the person(s) whose name(s) is/are sub-scribed to the within instrument and acknowledged to me that he/she/they executed the same in his/her/their authorized capacity(ies), and that by his/her/their signature(s) on the instrument the person(s), or the entity upon behalf of which the person(s) acted, executed the instrument. WITNESS my hand and official seal.

Signature_____   Affiant _____Known _____Unknown
                                                            ID Produced_____
                                                                                          (Seal)

_____
Signature of Preparer

_____
Address of Preparer

_____
Print name of Preparer

_____
City, State, Zip

MORTGAGE COMPARISON SHEET

Company name _____   **Phone number** _____

Annual Percentage Rate

    APR _____   (includes closing costs)

Terms

    ❒ 15-year ❒ 20-year ❒ 30-year ❒ Other _____

Type of Mortgage

❒ **Adjustable**

    Index _____   Margin over index

    Rate cap

    Adjustment period _____   Lifetime _____

    Conversion to fixed-rate

    When can it be converted? _____   How is conversion rate determined?

    What are the conditions? _____   Is there a conversion fee?

❒ **Fixed-rate** _____

    Interest Rate

    Lock in   During application   At approval   For

    How long   Lock-in cost

Points

    Points _____ ($_____)   Can points be amortized? ❒ Yes ❒ No

Down payment

    Minimum _____   Minimum without PMI _____

    Can down payment be financed? ❒ Yes ❒ No

Closing costs

    Application fee _____   Refundable? ❒ Yes ❒ No

    Loan origination fee _____   Title search/insurance _____

    Survey fee _____   Appraisal _____

    Transfer tax _____   Credit report fee _____

    Lender's attorney fee _____   Other fees _____

Loan processing time

    Application to approval _____ days   Approval to closing _____ days

MORTGAGE DEED

This Mortgage is given by   , hereinafter called Borrower, of
to   , hereinafter called Lender, which term includes any holder of this Mortgage, to secure the payment of the PRINCIPAL SUM of $ together with interest thereon computed on the outstanding balance, all as provided in a Note having the same date as this Mortgage, and also to secure the performance of all the terms, covenants, agreements, conditions and extensions of the Note and this Mortgage.

In consideration of the loan made by Lender to Borrower and for the purpose expressed above, the Borrower does hereby grant and convey to Lender, with MORTGAGE COVENANTS, the land with the buildings situated thereon and all the improvements and fixtures now and hereafter a part thereof, being more particularly described in Exhibit A attached hereto and made a part hereof and having a street address of:

_____

Attach Property Description

Borrower further covenants and agrees that:

1. No superior mortgage or the note secured by it will be modified without the consent of Lender hereunder.

2. Borrower will make with each periodic payment due under the Note secured by this Mortgage a payment sufficient to provide a fund from which the real estate taxes, betterment assessments and other municipal charges which can become a lien against the mortgaged premises can be paid by Lender when due. This provision shall be effective only in the event that a fund for the same purpose is not required to be established by the holder of a senior mortgage.

3. In the event that Borrower fails to carry out the covenants and agreements set forth herein, the Lender may do and pay for whatever is necessary to protect the value of and the Lender's rights in the mortgaged property and any amounts so paid shall be added to the Principal Sum due the Lender hereunder.

4. As additional security hereunder, Borrower hereby assigns to Lender, Borrower's rents of the mortgaged property, and upon default the same may be collected without the necessity of making entry upon the mortgaged premises.

5. In the event that any condition of this Mortgage or any senior mortgage shall be in default for fifteen (15) days, the entire debt shall become immediately due and payable at the option of the Lender. Lender shall be entitled to collect all costs and expenses, including reasonable attorney's fees incurred.

6. In the event that the Borrower transfers ownership (either legal or equitable) or any security interest in the mortgaged property, whether voluntarily or involuntarily, the Lender may at its option declare the entire debt due and payable.

7. This Mortgage is also security for all other direct and contingent liabilities of the Borrower to Lender which are due or become due and whether now existing or hereafter contracted.

8. Borrower shall maintain adequate insurance on the property in amounts and form of coverage acceptable to Lender and the Lender shall be a named insured as its interest may appear.

9. Borrower shall not commit waste or permit others to commit actual, permissive or constructive waste on the property.

10. Borrower further covenants and warrants to Lender that Borrower is indefeasibly seized of said land in fee simple; that the Borrower has lawful authority to mortgage said land and that said land is free and clear of all encumbrances except as may be expressly contained herein.

This Mortgage is upon the STATUTORY CONDITION and the other conditions set forth herein, for breach of which Lender shall have the STATUTORY POWER OF SALE to the extent existing under State law.

Executed under seal this _____ day of _____ , _____ (year).

_____   _____
Borrower   Borrower

STATE OF _____   }
COUNTY OF _____   }

On _____ before me, _____ , personally appeared _____ , personally known to me (or proved to me on the basis of satisfactory evidence) to be the person(s) whose name(s) is/are subscribed to the within instrument and acknowledged to me that he/she/they executed the same in his/her/their authorized capacity(ies), and that by his/her/their signature(s) on the instrument the person(s), or the entity upon behalf of which the person(s) acted, executed the instrument. WITNESS my hand and official seal.

Signature_____

Affiant _____Known _____Unknown
ID Produced_____
(Seal)

_____   _____
Signature of Preparer   Address of Preparer

_____   _____
Print name of Preparer   City, State, Zip

OFFER TO PURCHASE REAL ESTATE

BE IT KNOWN, the undersigned   of

(Buyer) offers to purchase from   of

(Owner), real estate known as   ,

City/Town of   , County of   , State of

, said property more particularly described as:

and containing   square feet of land, more or less.

The purchase price is	$
Deposit herewith paid	$
Upon signing sales agreement	$
Balance at closing	$_____
Total purchase price	$

This offer is subject to Buyer obtaining a real estate mortgage for no less than

$ payable over   years with interest not to exceed   %   at

customary terms within   days from date hereof.

The broker to this transaction is   who shall be paid a com-

mission of   by seller upon closing.

This offer is further subject to Buyer obtaining a satisfactory home inspection report and

termite/pest report within   days from date hereof.

Said property is to be sold free and clear of all encumbrances, by good and marketable

title, with full possession of said property available to Buyer.

The parties agree to execute a standard purchase and sales agreement according to the

terms of this agreement within   days.

The closing shall be on or before   ,   (year), at the deed recording office.

Signed this   day of   ,   (year).

In the presence of:

_____

Witness

_____

Witness

_____

Broker

_____

Buyer

_____

Owner

OPEN LISTING REALTY AGREEMENT

1.   This agreement signed on the   day of   ,   (year), by and between   (Owner) and

                    (Real Estate Broker) who agree as follows:

2.   Listing term. Owner lists the property described in Paragraph 3, with the Real Estate Broker for a period of   days, from date hereof.

3.   Description of Property. The property listed is located at

4.   Commission. The Owner agrees to pay the Real Estate Broker a commission of   % of the sale price should the Broker find a purchaser ready, willing, and able to pay at least $ for the property or such other sum as may be accepted by Owner. Said commissions are payable upon closing.

5.   Non-Exclusive. The Owner retains the right to sell the property directly on his or her own behalf with no sales commission to broker, so long as the Broker did not find this purchaser. The Owner further has the right to list the property with other brokers. If a sale is made within   months after this agreement terminates to parties found by the Real Estate Agent during the term of this agreement, and wherein the buyer has been disclosed to the Owner, the Owner shall pay the commission specified above.

6.   Forfeit of Deposit. If a deposit of money is forfeited by a purchaser produced by Broker, one half shall be retained by the Broker, providing that this amount does not exceed the commission, and one half shall be paid to the Owner.

Witnessed:

_____   _____
Witness   Owner

_____   _____
Witness   Broker

PERSONAL FINANCIAL WORKSHEET

Name:_____ Date: _____

Assets:

Cash	$_____
Checking Account(s)	$_____
Savings Account(s)	$_____
Other Savings (CDs, etc.)	$_____
Home (market value)	$_____
Other Real Estate (market value)	$_____
Household Furnishings (market value)	$_____
Automobile(s) (blue book value)	$_____
Life Insurance (cash value)	$_____
Stocks, Bonds (current value)	$_____
Retirement Plans/Profit Sharing	$_____
Other Assets	$_____
Total Assets:	**$_____**

Debts:

Mortgages (balance due)	$_____
Installment Loans (balance due)	$_____
Other Loans (balance due)	$_____
Credit Cards (balance due)	$_____
Charge Accounts (amount owed)	$_____
Insurance Premiums Due	$_____
Taxes Owed to Date	$_____
Other Debts	$_____
Total Debts:	**$_____**
Net Worth (Total Assets minus Total Debts):	**$_____**

PROPERTY FACT WORKSHEET

Address _____

Owner name _____ Phone _____

Asking price _____

Appraisal price _____

Taxes _____

Year of completion _____

Location _____

Lot size _____

Interior space _____ sq. ft.

Style _____

Bedrooms: no., size _____

Bathrooms: no., size _____

Foundation _____

Siding _____

Roof _____

Exterior Windows & Doors _____

Garage/Shed _____

Parking Area _____

Public Utilities _____

Heating/Cooling systems _____

Fireplace _____

Insulation _____

Floor coverings _____

Wall coverings _____

Closets and storage space _____

Kitchen size, style _____

Dining room _____

Living room/Family room _____

Den/Study _____

Laundry room _____

Porch/Deck _____

Appliances _____

Expansion potential _____

Other _____

Other _____

QUITCLAIM DEED

THIS QUITCLAIM DEED, Executed this   day of   ,
(year),

by first party, Grantor,

whose post office address is

to second party, Grantee,

whose post office address is

WITNESSETH, That the said first party, for good consideration and for the sum of
                                   Dollars ($) paid by the said second
party, the receipt whereof is hereby acknowledged, does hereby remise, release and quitclaim
unto the said second party forever, all the right, title, interest and claim which the said first party
has in and to the following described parcel of land, and improvements and appurtenances thereto in the County of   , State of   to wit:

IN WITNESS WHEREOF, The said first party has signed and sealed these presents the day and year first above written. Signed, sealed and delivered in presence of:

_____
Signature of Witness

_____
Print name of Witness

_____
Signature of Witness

_____
Print name of Witness

_____
Signature of First Party

_____
Print name of First Party

_____
Signature of First Party

_____
Print name of First Party

State of   }
County of
On   before me,   ,
appeared
personally known to me (or proved to me on the basis of satisfactory evidence) to be the person(s) whose name(s) is/are subscribed to the within instrument and acknowledged to me that he/she/they executed the same in his/her/their authorized capacity(ies), and that by his/her/their signature(s) on the instrument the person(s), or the entity upon behalf of which the person(s) acted, executed the instrument.
WITNESS my hand and official seal.

_____
Signature of Notary

Affiant _____Known_____Produced ID
Type of ID _____
                                   (Seal)

State of   }
County of
On   before me,   ,
appeared
personally known to me (or proved to me on the basis of satisfactory evidence) to be the person(s) whose name(s) is/are subscribed to the within instrument and acknowledged to me that he/she/they executed the same in his/her/their authorized capacity(ies), and that by his/her/their signature(s) on the instrument the person(s), or the entity upon behalf of which the person(s) acted, executed the instrument.
WITNESS my hand and official seal.

_____
Signature of Notary

Affiant _____Known_____Produced ID
Type of ID _____
                                   (Seal)

_____
Signature of Preparer

_____
Print name of Preparer

_____
Address of Preparer

_____
City, State, Zip

REALTOR CHECKLIST

Name of Realtor: _____

_____

Company: _____

_____

Phone No./Fax: _____

_____

Time with company: _____

_____

Related experience: _____

_____

Why residential: _____

_____

Future goals: _____

_____

Contract Terms: _____

_____

Fee: _____

_____

Personality: _____

_____

References: _____

_____

Other Comments: _____

_____

RELEASE AND WAIVER OF OPTION RIGHTS

The undersigned is purchaser of an option to purchase and acquire real property dated _____ , _____ (year), executed by _____ as seller, and recorded _____ on _____ , _____ (year), in volume _____ , on page _____ , of the deed records of _____ County, State of _____ .

The option expired on _____ , _____ (year).

Purchaser, the sole owner and holder of the option, acknowledges that the same was not exercised prior to the expiration date, and since that date the option has been and is now void and of no effect. Purchaser hereby waives and releases all claim, right, and interest in the option, and in the real property therein described.

IN WITNESS WHEREOF, this instrument has been executed on _____ , _____ (year).

_____

STATE OF _____ }
COUNTY OF _____

On _____ before me, _____ , personally appeared _____ , personally known to me (or proved to me on the basis of satisfactory evidence) to be the person(s) whose name(s) is/are sub-scribed to the within instrument and acknowledged to me that he/she/they executed the same in his/her/their authorized capacity(ies), and that by his/her/their signature(s) on the instrument the person(s), or the entity upon behalf of which the person(s) acted, executed the instrument. WITNESS my hand and official seal.

Signature_____

Affiant _____Known _____Unknown
ID Produced_____
(Seal)

_____
Signature of Preparer

_____
Address of Preparer

_____
Print name of Preparer

_____
City, State, Zip

RELEASE OF CONTRACT

We hereby mutually agree that the contract of sale executed and dated _____

between _____ (Buyers)

and _____ (Sellers)

is null and void. Buyers and Sellers shall have no rights, claims, or liabilities thereunder and each

of them specifically waives any claims or rights he may have against any of the others. We fur-

ther authorize _____(escrow agent)

to release earnest money deposited to the Buyers in the amount of _____

_____ ($ _____).

_____   _____

Seller   Date

_____   _____

Seller   Date

_____   _____

Buyer   Date

_____   _____

Buyer   Date

RELEASE OF MORTGAGE BY A CORPORATION

_____, a corporation incorporated under the laws of the State of _____, having its principal office at _____, hereby certifies that the mortgage, dated _____, (year), executed by _____, as mortgagor, to _____ as mortgagee, and recorded _____, (year), in the office of the _____ of the County of _____, State of _____, in the Book of mortgages, page _____, together with the debt secured by said mortgage, has been fully paid, satisfied, released, and discharged, and that the property secured thereby has been released from the lien of such mortgage.

IN WITNESS WHEREOF, _____ has caused this release to be duly signed by its _____ authorized to sign by the resolution of its board of directors and caused its corporate seal to be affixed hereto on _____, (year).

_____

Title:_____

STATE OF
COUNTY OF   }

On _____ before me, _____, personally appeared _____, personally known to me (or proved to me on the basis of satisfactory evidence) to be the person(s) whose name(s) is/are subscribed to the within instrument and acknowledged to me that he/she/they executed the same in his/her/their authorized capacity(ies), and that by his/her/their signature(s) on the instrument the person(s), or the entity upon behalf of which the person(s) acted, executed the instrument. WITNESS my hand and official seal.

Signature_____

Affiant   _____Known   _____Unknown
ID Produced_____
(Seal)

_____   _____
Signature of Preparer   Address of Preparer

RESIDENTIAL LOAN APPLICATION

MORTGAGE APPLIED FOR →	☐ Conventional ☐ VA ☐ FHA ☐	Amount $	Interest	No. of Months	Monthly Payment Principal & Interest	Escrow/impounds (to be collected monthly) ☐ Taxes ☐ Hazard Ins. ☐ Mtg. Ins. ☐

Prepayment Option

SUBJECT PROPERTY

Property Street Address		City	County	State	Zip	No. of Units

Legal Description (Attach description if necessary)	Year Built

Purpose of Loan: ☐ Purchase ☐ Construction-Permanent ☐ Construction-Refinance ☐ Other (Explain)

Complete this line if Construction-Permanent or Construction-Loan →	Lot Value Data Year Acquired	Original Cost $	Present Value (a) $	Cost of Imp. (b) $	Total (a + b) $	Enter Total as purchase price in details ← of purchase

Complete this line if a Refinance Loan		Purpose of Refinance	Describe Improvements ( ) made ( ) to be made
Year Acquired	Original Cost $	Amt. Existing Liens $	Cost: $

Name(s) Title Will Be Held In	Manner In Which Title Will Be Held

Source of Down Payment and Settlement Charges

This application is designed to be completed by the borrower(s) with the lender's assistance. The Co-Borrower Section and all other Co-Borrower questions must be completed and the appropriate boxes checked if ☐ another person will be jointly obligated with the Borrower on the loan, or ☐ the Borrower is relying on income from alimony, child support or separate maintenance or on the income or assets of another person as a basis for repayment of the loan, or ☐ the Borrower is married and resides, or the property is located, in a community property state.

BORROWER				CO-BORROWER			
Name		Age	School Yrs.	Name		Age	School Yrs.
Present Address No. Years_____ ☐ Own ☐ Rent				**Present Address** No. Years_____ ☐ Own ☐ Rent			
Street _____				Street _____			
City/State/Zip_____				City/State/Zip_____			
Former Address if less than 2 years at present address				**Former Address** if less than 2 years at present address			
Street _____				Street _____			
City/State/Zip_____				City/State/Zip_____			
Years at former address _____ ☐ Own ☐ Rent				Years at former address _____ ☐ Own ☐ Rent			
Marital Status ☐ Married ☐ Separated ☐ Unmarried (incl. single, divorced, widowed)		Dependents other than listed by co-borrower No. Ages:		**Marital Status** ☐ Married ☐ Separated ☐ Unmarried (incl. single, divorced, widowed)		Dependents other than listed by co-borrower No. Ages:	
Name and Address of Employer		Years employed in this line of work or profession:_____ Years on the job:_____ ☐ Self Employed*		Name and Address of Employer		Years employed in this line of work or profession:_____ Years on the job:_____ ☐ Self Employed*	
Position/Title	Type of Business			Position/Title	Type of Business		
Social Security Number***	Home Phone	Business Phone		Social Security Number***	Home Phone	Business Phone	

GROSS MONTHLY INCOME

Item	Borrower	Co-Borrower	Total
Base Empl. Income	$	$	$
Overtime			
Bonuses			
Commissions			
Dividends/Interests			
Net Rental Income			
Other ♣ (Before completing, see notice under Describe Other Income below)			
Total	$	$	$

MONTHLY HOUSING EXPENSE**

Item	Present	Proposed
Rent	$	$
First Mortgage (P & I)		
Other Financing (P & I)		
Hazard Insurance		
Real Estate Taxes		
Mortgage Insurance		
Homeowner Assoc. Dues		
Other:		
Total Monthly Pmt.		
Utilities		
Total	$	$

DETAILS OF PURCHASE
Do Not Complete If Refinance

a. Purchase Price	$
b. Total Closing Costs (Est.)	
c. Prepaid Escrows (Est.)	
d. Total (a + b + c)	$
e. Amount This Mortgage	
f. Other Financing	
g. Other Equity	
h. Amount of Cash Deposit	
i. Closing Costs Paid by Seller	
j. Cash Req. for Closing (Est.)	

DESCRIBE OTHER INCOME

↓ B = Borrower   C = Co-Borrower   NOTICE: ♣ Alimony, child support, or separate maintenance income need not be revealed if the Borrower or Co-Borrower does not choose to have it considered as basis for repaying this loan.

	Monthly Amount
	$

IF EMPLOYED IN CURRENT POSITION FOR LESS THAN TWO YEARS COMPLETE THE FOLLOWING

B/C	Previous Employer/School	City/State	Type of Business	Position/Title	Dates From/To	Monthly Income

THESE QUESTIONS APPLY TO BOTH BORROWER AND CO-BORROWER

If a "yes" answer is given to a question in this column, please explain on an attached sheet.	Borrower Yes or No	Co-Borrower Yes or No		Borrower Yes or No	Co-Borrower Yes or No
Are there any outstanding judgments against you?	_____	_____	Are you a co-maker or endorser on a note?	_____	_____
Have you been declared bankrupt within the past 7 years?	_____	_____	Are you a U.S. citizen?	_____	_____
Have you had property disclosed upon or given title or deed in lieu thereof in the last 7 years?	_____	_____	If "no," are you a resident alien?	_____	_____
Are you a party to a lawsuit?	_____	_____	If "no," are you a non-resident alien?	_____	_____
Are you obliged to pay alimony, child support, or separate maintenance?	_____	_____	Explain Other Financing or Other Equity (if any). _____		
Is any part of the down payment borrowed?	_____	_____			

* FHLMC/FNMA require business credit report, signed Federal Income Tax returns for the last two years, and, if available, audited Profit and Loss Statement plus balance sheet for same period.
** All present Monthly Housing Expenses of Borrower and Co-Borrower should be listed on a combined basis.
***Optional for FHLMC.

163

STATEMENT OF ASSETS AND LIABILITIES

This Statement and any applicable supporting schedules may be completed jointly by both married and unmarried couples as owners if their assets and liabilities are sufficiently joined so that the Statement can be meaningfully and fairly represented on a combined basis; otherwise separate Statements and Schedules are required (FHLMC 65A/FNMA 1003A). If the co-borrower section was completed about a spouse, this statement and supporting schedules must be completed about that spouse also. ❑ Completed Jointly ❑ Not Completed Jointly

ASSETS		LIABILITIES AND PLEDGED ASSETS			
Description	Cash or Market Value	Creditor's Name, Address and Account Number	Acct. Name if Not Borrower's	Mo. Pmt. and Mos. Left to Pay	Unpaid Balance
Cash Deposit Toward Purchase Held By		Installment Debts (Include "revolving" charge accounts) Co. Address City	Acct. No.	$ Pmt./Mos.	$
Checking and Savings Accounts (Show Names of Institutions and Account Numbers) **Bank, S & L or Credit Union** Address City Acct. No.		Co. Address City	Acct. No.		
		Co. Address City	Acct. No.		
Bank, S & L or Credit Union Address City Acct. No.		Co. Address City	Acct. No.		
		Other Debts Including Stock Pledges			
Stocks and Bonds (No./Description)		Real Estate Loans Co. Address City	Acct. No.		
Life Insurance Net Cash Value Face Amount $		Co. Address City	Acct. No.		
Subtotal Liquid Assets					
Real Estate Owned (Enter Market Value from Schedule of Real Estate Owned)		Automobile Loans Co. Address City	Acct. No.		
Vested Interest in Retirement Fund					
Net Worth of Businesses Owned (ATTACH FINANCIAL STATEMENT)		Co. Address City	Acct. No.		
Automobile Owned (Make and Year)					
Furniture and Personal Property					
Other Assets (itemize)		Alimony/Child Support/Separate Maintenance Payments Owed to			
		Total Monthly Payments		$	
Total Assets	A $	Net Worth (A minus B) $		Total Liabilities	B $

SCHEDULE OF REAL ESTATE OWNED (if Additional Properties Owned Attach Separate Schedule)

Address of Property (indicate S if Sold, PS if Pending Sale, or R if Rental being held for income) ↓	Type of Property	Present Market Value	Amount of Mortgages & Liens	Gross Rental Income	Mortgage Payments	Taxes, Ins. Maintenance, Misc.	Net Rental Income
		$	$	$	$	$	$
TOTALS →		$	$	$	$	$	$

LIST PREVIOUS CREDIT REFERENCES

B=Borrower C=Co-Borrower	Creditor's Name and Address	Account Number	Purpose	Highest Balance	Date Paid
				$	

List any additional names under which credit has previously been received:

AGREEMENT: The undersigned applies for the loan indicated in this application to be secured by a first mortgage or deed of trust on the property described herein, and represents that the property will not be used for any illegal or restricted purpose, and that all statements made in this application are true and are made for the purpose of obtaining the loan. Verification may be obtained from any source named in this application. The original or a copy of this application will be retained by the lender, even if the loan is not granted. The undersigned ❑ intend or ❑ do not intend to occupy the property as their primary residence.

I/we fully understand that it is a federal crime punishable by fine or imprisonment, or both, to knowingly make any false statements concerning any of the above facts as applicable under the provisions of Title 18, United States Code, Section 1014.

_____ Date _____   _____ Date _____
Borrower's Signature   Co-Borrower's Signature

INFORMATION FOR GOVERNMENT MONITORING PURPOSES

The following information is requested by the Federal Government for certain types of loans related to a dwelling, in order to monitor the lender's compliance with equal credit opportunity and fair housing laws. You are not required to furnish this information, but are encouraged to do so. The law provides that a lender may neither discriminate on the basis of this information, nor on whether you choose to furnish it. However, if you choose not to furnish it, under Federal regulations this lender is required to note race and sex on the basis of visual observation and surname. If you do not wish to furnish the above information, please check the box below. (Lender must review the above material to assure that the disclosures satisfy all requirements to which the lender is subject under applicable state law for the particular type of loan applied for.

Borrower: ❑ I do not wish to furnish this information   Co-Borrower: ❑ I do not wish to furnish this information
Race/National Origin: Race/National Origin:
❑ American Indian, Alaskan Native ❑ Asian, Pacific Islander   ❑ American Indian, Alaskan Native ❑ Asian, Pacific Islander
❑ Black ❑ Hispanic ❑ White   ❑ Black ❑ Hispanic ❑ White
❑ Other (specify): _____   ❑ Other (specify): _____
Sex: ❑ Female ❑ Male   Sex: ❑ Female ❑ Male

TO BE COMPLETED BY INTERVIEWER

This application was taken by:
❑ face to face interview
❑ by mail
❑ by telephone

_____   _____
Interviewer   Name of Interviewer's Employer

_____   _____
Interviewer's Phone Number   Address of Interviewer's Employer

TRUTH-IN-LENDING DISCLOSURE STATEMENT

Borrower's Name (Last-First-Middle Initial) and Address (Street-City-State-Zip Code)	Date	Loan Number
	Lender Name	

TRUTH-IN-LENDING DISCLOSURE

ANNUAL PERCENTAGE RATE	FINANCE CHARGE	AMOUNT FINANCED	TOTAL OF PAYMENTS	*=ESTIMATED
The cost of your credit as a yearly rate	The dollar amount the credit will cost you	The amount of credit provided to you or on your behalf	The amount you will have paid when you have made all payments as scheduled	
%	$	$	$	

Payment Schedule	Total Payments	Filing/Recording Fees: $

Number of Payments   Amount of Payments (Principal & Interest & Private Mortgage Insurance, if applicable)   When Payments are Due

ADJUSTABLE RATE FEATURE:

_____ This loan does not have an adjustable rate feature.

_____ This loan has an adjustable rate feature. Disclosures about the adjustable rate feature have been provided to you earlier.

SECURITY: You are giving a security interest in the property located at:

LATE CHARGES: If your payment is more than _____ days delinquent, a late charge of ____% of the monthly principal and interest payment will be assessed.

ASSUMPTION: Someone buying your home

_____ Cannot assume the remainder of the mortgage on the original terms

_____ May, subject to conditions, be allowed to assume the remainder of the mortgage on the original terms.

PREPAYMENT: If you payoff early, you

_____ may _____ will not have to pay a penalty

_____ may _____ will not be entitled to a refund of part of the refinance charge.

See your contract documents for any additional information regarding non-payment, default, required re-payment in full before scheduled date and payment refunds and penalties.

INSURANCE: Hazard insurance in the amount of $_____ and flood insurance in the amount of $_____ with loss payable clause to the lender required as a condition of this loan. This insurance may be purchased from any insurance company of the Borrower's choice who is acceptable to the Lender.

Credit life or disability insurance is not required in connection with this transaction. If such coverage is desired, it may be purchased through any person of Borrower's choice or it is available through Lender upon submission of a separate application. This insurance is not in effect and no charge is made for such coverage until a separate application has been submitted and approved.

ITEMIZATION OF THE AMOUNT FINANCED

Loan Amount	Prepaid Finance Charge	Note Interest Rate	Loan Type
$	$		

I/We hereby acknowledge reading and receiving a complete copy of this disclosure along with copies of documents referred to in this disclosure.

_____   _____   _____   _____
Borrower/Signature   Date   Co-Borrower/Signature   Date

165

RESIDENTIAL REAL ESTATE SALES DISCLOSURE

THE PROSPECTIVE BUYER AND THE OWNER MAY WISH TO OBTAIN PROFESSIONAL ADVICE OR INSPECTIONS OF THE PROPERTY AND PROVIDE FOR APPROPRIATE PROVISIONS IN A CONTRACT BETWEEN THEM CONCERNING ANY ADVICE, INSPECTIONS, DEFECTS, OR WARRANTIES OBTAINED ON THE PROPERTY. THE REPRESENTATIONS IN THIS FORM ARE REPRESENTATIONS OF THE OWNER AND ARE NOT REPRESENTATIONS OF THE AGENT, IF ANY. THIS INFORMATION IS FOR DISCLOSURE ONLY AND IS NOT INTENDED TO BE A PART OF THE CONTRACT BETWEEN THE BUYER AND OWNER.

Seller states that the information contained in this Disclosure is correct as of the date below, to the best of the Seller's current actual knowledge.

DATE _____ PROPERTY ADDRESS _____

The Condition of the Following Property Is:	N/A	Defective	Not Defective	Unknown
1. ELECTRICAL SYSTEM				
a) Air filtration system				
b) Burglar alarm				
c) Cable TV wiring and connections				
d) Ceiling fans				
e) Garage door opener				
f) Inside telephone wiring and jacks				
g) Intercom				
h) Kitchen range hood				
i) Light fixtures				
j) Sauna				
k) Smoke/fire alarm				
l) Switches and outlets				
m) Amp services				
n) Other				
2. HEATING AND COOLING				
a) Attic fan				
b) Central air conditioning				
c) Hot water heater				
d) Furnace heater-gas, electric, oil, solar				
e) Fireplace				
f) Humidifier				
g) Propane tank				
h) Other				
3. APPLIANCES				
a) Vacuum system (built-in)				
b) Clothes washing machine				
c) Clothes dryer				
d) Compactor				
e) Convection oven				
f) Dishwasher				
g) Freezer				
h) Garbage disposal				
i) Gas grill				
j) Microwave oven				
k) Oven				
l) Range				
m) Refrigerator				
n) TV antenna/dish				
o) Other				

	N/A	DEFECTIVE	NOT DEFECTIVE	UNKNOWN
4. WATER & SEWER SYSTEM				
a) Cistern				
b) Septic field/bed				
c) Hot tub				
d) Plumbing				
e) Aerator system				
f) Sump pump				
g) Sprinkler /irrigation system				
h) Water heater-gas, electric, solar				
i) Water filtration system				
j) Water softener				
k) Well				
l) Public water system				
m) Public sewer system				
n) Private/community water system				
o) Private/community sewer system				
p) Other systems				

	YES	NO	UNKNOWN
5. FOUNDATION & STRUCTURE			
a) Are there any problems with the foundation?			
b) Are there any structural problems with the building?			
c) Have any substantial additions or alterations been made without a required building permit?			
d) Are there any violations of zoning, building codes or restrictive covenants?			
e) Are there moisture or water problems?			
f) Is there termite, rodent or insect damage?			
g) Is there damage due to wind or flood?			
h) Is the property in a flood plain?			
i) Is the property located within 1 (one) nautical mile of an airport?			
j) Is there any threat of or pending litigation regarding the property?			
k) Are the furnace, wood stove, chimney/flue in working order?			
6. ROOF			
a) Age in years_____			
b) Are there any current leaks?			
c) Is roof currently damaged?			
d) Is there more than one roof on the structure? If yes, how many_____?			

7. HAZARDOUS CONDITIONS

Are there any existing hazards on the property such as methane gas, radioactive material, radon or lead paint in house or well, or expansive soil, toxic materials, asbestos insulation, landfill, mineshaft or PCBs? If yes, explain:

8. Additional comments or explanations:

Seller and Buyer hereby acknowledge receipt of this Disclosure Form by signing below:

Seller's Signature	Date	Buyer's Signature	Date
Seller's Name		Buyer's Name	
Seller's Signature	Date	Buyer's Signature	Date
Seller's Name		Buyer's Name	

SCHEDULE OF PROGRESS - BUYER

TASK	TARGET DATE	COMPLETION DATE
Review Ads	_____	_____
Visit Homes	_____	_____
Make an Offer	_____	_____
Sign Disclosure	_____	_____
Sign Contract	_____	_____
Deposit earnest money	_____	_____
Get home inspected	_____	_____
Resolve contingencies	_____	_____
Apply for loan	_____	_____
Loan sent to underwriting	_____	_____
Receive loan approval	_____	_____
Send commitment letter	_____	_____
Complete title work	_____	_____
Get home appraised	_____	_____
Receive appraisal results	_____	_____
Obtain hazard insurance	_____	_____
Settlement - closing statement	_____	_____

SCHEDULE OF PROGRESS - SELLER

TASK	TARGET DATE	COMPLETION DATE
Place Ad	_____	_____
Open House	_____	_____
Review Offers	_____	_____
Submit Disclosure	_____	_____
Sign Contract	_____	_____
Deposit earnest money	_____	_____
Buyer's Inspection	_____	_____
Resolve contingencies	_____	_____
Buyer applies for loan	_____	_____
Buyer loan approved	_____	_____
Receive commitment letter	_____	_____
Complete title work	_____	_____
Appraisal date	_____	_____
Receive appraisal results	_____	_____
Settlement - closing statement	_____	_____

A. **Settlement Statement**

B. Type of Loan		6. File Number	7. Loan Number	8. Mortgage Insurance Case Number

C. NOTE: This form is furnished to give you a statement of actual settlement costs. Amounts paid to and by the settlement agent are shown. Items marked "(p.o.c.)" were paid outside the closing; they are shown here for informational purposes and are not included in the totals.

D. Name and Address of Borrower	E. Name and Address of Seller	F. Name and Address of Lender
		H. Settlement Agent
G. Property Location	Place of Settlement	
	I. SETTLEMENT DATE:	

J. SUMMARY OF BORROWER'S TRANSACTION			
100. GROSS AMOUNT DUE FROM BORROWER		207.	
101. Contract sales price		208.	
102. Personal property		209.	
103. Settlement charges to borrower (line 1400)		209a	
104.		209b	
105.		Adjustments for items unpaid by seller	
Adjustments for items paid by seller in advance		210. City/town taxes to	
106. City/town taxes to		211. County taxes to	
107. County taxes to		212. Assessments to	
108. Assessments to		213.	
109.		214.	
110.		215.	
111.		216.	
112.		217.	
120. GROSS AMOUNT DUE FROM BORROWER		218.	
		219.	
200. AMOUNTS PAID BY OR IN BEHALF OF BORROWER		**220. TOTAL AMOUNTS PAID BY OR IN BEHALF OF BORROWER**	
201. Deposit or earnest money		**300. CASH AT SETTLEMENT FROM/TO BORROWER**	
202. Principal amount of new loan(s)		301. Gross amount due from borrower (line 120)	
203. Existing loan(s) taken subject to		302. Less amounts paid by/for borrower (line 220)	( )
204.		303. CASH ❑ From ❑ To **BORROWER**	
205.			
206.			

K. SUMMARY OF SELLER'S TRANSACTION

400. GROSS AMOUNT DUE TO SELLER		507.	
401. Contract sales price		508.	
402. Personal property		509.	
403.		509a	
404.		509b	
405.		Adjustments for items unpaid by seller	
Adjustments for items paid by seller in advance		510. City/town taxes to	
406. City/town taxes to		511. County taxes to	
407. County taxes to		512. Assessments to	
408. Assessments to		513.	
409.		514.	
410.		515.	
411.		516.	
412.		517.	
420. GROSS AMOUNT DUE TO SELLER		518.	
500. REDUCTIONS IN AMOUNT DUE TO SELLER		519.	
		520. TOTAL REDUCTIONS IN AMOUNT DUE SELLER	
501. Excess deposit (see instructions)		600. CASH AT SETTLEMENT TO/FROM SELLER	
502. Settlement charges to seller (line 1400)		601. Gross amount due to seller (line 420)	
503. Existing loan(s) taken subject to		602. Less reductions in amount due seller (line 520)	( )
504. Payoff of first mortgage loan		603. CASH ❏ To ❏ From **SELLER**	
505.			
506. Payoff of second mortgage loan			

L. Settlement Charges		Paid From Borrower's Funds At Settlement	Paid From Seller's Funds At Settlement
700. TOTAL SALES/BROKER'S COM. based on price $ @ % =			
Division of Commission (line 700) as follows:			
701. $ to			
702. $ to			
703. Commission paid at Settlement			
704.			
800. Items Payable In Connection With Loan			
801. Loan Origination Fee %			
802. Loan Discount %			
803. Appraisal Fee to			
804. Credit Report to			
805. Lender's Inspection Fee			
806.			
807.			
808.			
809.			
810.			
811.			
900. Items Required By Lender To Be Paid In Advance			
901. Interest from to @ $ /day			
902. Mortgage Insurance Premium for months to			
903. Hazard Insurance Premium for years to			
904.			
905.			

1000.	**Reserves Deposited With Lender**				
1001.	Hazard Insurance	months@ $	per month		
1002.	Mortgage Insurance	months@ $	per month		
1003.	City Property Taxes	months@ $	per month		
1004.	County Property Taxes	months@ $	per month		
1005.	Annual Assessments	months@ $	per month		
1006.		months@ $	per month		
1007.		months@ $	per month		
1008.		months@ $	per month		
1100.	**Title Charges**				
1101.	Settlement or closing fee	to			
1102.	Abstract or title search	to			
1103.	Title examination	to			
1104.	Title insurance binder	to			
1105.	Document preparation	to			
1106.	Notary fees	to			
1107.	Attorney's fees				
	(includes above items numbers:			)	
1108.	Title insurance: Risk Premium				
	(includes above items numbers:			)	
1109.	Lender's coverage: Risk Premium $				
1110.	Owner's coverage: Risk Premium $				
1110a	Endorsements:				
1111.					
1112.					
1113.					
1200.	**Government Recording and Transfer Charges**				
1201.	Recording fees: Deed $	Mortgage(s) $	Releases $		
1202.	City/county tax/stamps: Deed $	Mortgage(s) $			
1203.	State tax/stamps: Deed $	Mortgage(s) $			
1204.					
1205.					
1300.	**Additional Settlement Charges**				
1301.	Survey	to			
1302.	Pest inspection	to			
1303.					
1304.					
1305.					
1306.					
1307.					
1400.	**Total Settlement Charges** (enter on lines 103, Section J and 502, Section K)	⇨			

CERTIFICATION

I have carefully reviewed the Settlement Statement and to the best of my knowledge and belief, it is a true and accurate statement of all receipts and disbursements made on my account or by me in this transaction. I further certify that I have received a copy of the Settlement Statement.

_____ Borrower   _____ Seller

_____ Borrower   _____ Seller

The Settlement Statement which I have prepared is a true and accurate account of this transaction. I have caused, or will cause, the funds to be disbursed in accordance with this statement.

_____ Settlement Agent   _____ Date

WARNING: It is a crime to knowingly make false statements to the United States on this or any other similar form. Penalties upon conviction can include a fine and imprisonment. For details see: Title 18 U.S. Code Section 1001 and Section 1010.

WARRANTY DEED

For good consideration, we

of   , County of   , State of

, hereby bargain, deed and convey to   of

, County of   , State of

, the following described land in   County, free

and clear with WARRANTY COVENANTS; to wit:

Grantor(s), for itself and its heirs, hereby covenants with Grantee, its heirs, and assigns, that Grantor(s) is lawfully seized in fee simple of the above-described premises; that it has a good right to convey; that the premises are free from all encumbrances; that Grantor(s) and its heirs, and all persons acquiring any interest in the property granted, through or for Grantor(s), will, on demand of Grantee, or its heirs or assigns, and at the expense of Grantee, its heirs or assigns, execute any instrument necessary for the further assurance of the title to the premises that may be reasonably required; and that Grantor(s) and its heirs will forever warrant and defend all of the property so granted to Grantee, its heirs, and assigns, against every person lawfully claiming the same or any part thereof.

Being the same property conveyed to the Grantor(s) by deed of   , dated

,   (year).

WITNESS the hands and seal of said Grantor(s) this   day of   ,   (year).

_____
Grantor

_____
Grantor

STATE OF   }
COUNTY OF

On   before me,   , personally appeared
                                                    , personally known to me (or
proved to me on the basis of satisfactory evidence) to be the person(s) whose name(s) is/are subscribed to the within instrument and acknowledged to me that he/she/they executed the same in
his/her/their authorized capacity(ies), and that by his/her/their signature(s) on the instrument the
person(s), or the entity upon behalf of which the person(s) acted, executed the instrument.
WITNESS my hand and official seal.

Signature_____   Affiant   _____Known   _____Unknown
                                                 ID Produced_____
                                                                                 (Seal)

_____
Signature of Preparer

_____
Print name of Preparer

_____
Address of Preparer

_____
City, State, Zip

HOMEOWNERS' ASSOCIATION DISCLOSURE SUMMARY

1)   This is a disclosure summary for _____ (name of community).

2)   As Purchaser of Property in this community, you will be obligated to be a member of a homeowners' association.

3)   There have been, or will be recorded, restrictive covenants governing the use and occupancy of properties in this community.

4)   You will be obligated to pay assessments to the association; these assessments are subject to periodic change.

5)   Your failure to pay these assessments could result in a lien on your property.

6)   There [check only one] ❏ is ❏ is not an obligation to pay rent or land use fees for recreational or other commonly used facilities as an obligation of membership in the homeowners' association. (If such obligation exists, then the amount of the current obligation is $_____.)

7)   The restrictive covenants [check only one] ❏ can ❏ cannot be amended without the approval of the association membership.

8)   The statements contained in this disclosure form are only summary in nature, and, as a prospective Purchaser, you should refer to the covenants and the association governing documents.

_____   _____
Date   Purchaser

                                                          _____
                                                          Purchaser

This disclosure must be supplied by the developer, or by the parcel owner if the sale is by an owner that is not the developer.

CONDOMINIUM ASSOCIATION DISCLOSURE SUMMARY

1)   This is a disclosure summary for _____ (name of community).

2)   As Purchaser of Property in this community, you will be obligated to be a member of a condominium association.

3)   There have been, or will be recorded, restrictive covenants governing the use and occupancy of properties in this community.

4)   You will be obligated to pay assessments to the association; these assessments are subject to periodic change.

5)   Your failure to pay these assessments could result in a lien on your property.

6)   There [check only one] ❑ is ❑ is not an obligation to pay rent or land use fees for recreational or other commonly used facilities as an obligation of membership in the condominium association. (If such obligation exists, then the amount of the current obligation is $_____.)

7)   The restrictive covenants [check only one] ❑ can ❑ cannot be amended without the approval of the association membership.

8)   The statements contained in this disclosure form are only summary in nature, and, as a prospective Purchaser, you should refer to the covenants and the association governing documents.

_____
Date

_____
Purchaser

_____
Purchaser

This disclosure must be supplied by the developer, or by the unit owner if the sale is by an owner that is not the developer.

PROPERTY VIEWING AND KEY AGREEMENT

With the signature below, I hereby acknowledge receipt of the key(s) to the dwelling located at:

_____.

I intend to use the key(s) for the express purpose of viewing the dwelling to decide if it is suitable for me to rent, and I will neither disturb nor remove anything found there. As a courtesy, I will report to the owner/manager anything that appears to be amiss at the dwelling.

I have given the owner/manager, whose acknowledgement appears below, a deposit of $_____, and also a valuable personal item consisting of _____ _____, both of which will be returned to me when I return the key(s).

I promise to return the key(s) by _____ (a.m.)(p.m.) TODAY to the owner/manager at the same place where I picked them up. Should I fail to do so, the owner/manager is entitled to keep the deposit to pay for changing the locks on the dwelling but will return my valuable personal item to me when asked.

I understand that this agreement gives me no occupancy rights whatsoever and that I must complete a rental application if I want to be considered as an applicant to rent this dwelling.

Signed: Current Address:

_____   _____

                                                 _____

Current Telephone Number: Date and Time:

_____ – _____ – _____   _____

Acknowledged by:

_____

(   ) Owner   (   ) Manager

Glossary of useful terms

Ad-As

Adjustable-rate mortgage

A mortgage in which the interest rate is adjusted over time, based on a given index.

Adjusted basis

The price paid for a principal residence minus the amount of any profit made from the sale of a previous home(s), according to the IRS.

Agent

A real estate representative who is usually an independent contractor working for a broker.

Amortization

To liquidate a debt by installment payments.

Annual percentage rate

The total rate of interest projected over the life of a loan.

Appraisal

An evaluation of a home/property that determines the current value of a home by comparing it to similar homes.

Assumption

When the buyer agrees to take over the obligations of the seller. If the buyer defaults, both the buyer and seller are responsible.

B-C

Balloon mortgage

A mortgage with an installment payment schedule, which also requires a lump sum payment(s) at a specific time.

Broker

A real estate representative who is licensed by the state.

Capital appreciation

The increase in market value of an asset such as a home, due to inflation or increased demand.

Clear title

Title to property for which public record shows no apparent encumbrances to the use and transfer of ownership or defects that would harm the buyer.

Closing

The procedure whereby title is transferred from seller to buyer; settlement.

Cloudy title

A dispute, lawsuit or other encumbrance which, if valid, affects the rights of the owner of the property.

Commission

A percentage of the sale price paid to a Realtor, broker or agent for services rendered.

Conventional mortgage

A home loan with a fixed rate.

Conveyance

The act of transferring a deed to another person.

C-E

Covenants

Clauses included in deeds or public records that prohibit or forebear specific acts.

Debt-to-income ratio

A ratio used by lenders to determine whether an applicant is qualified for a mortgage. It equals total amount of debt divided by total gross monthly income.

Deed

A document used to transfer title of real property.

Default

Failure to pay mortgage payments over a specified period of time.

Deposit

Good faith, earnest money down payment given by the buyer to the seller with an offer to purchase.

Disclosure

The legal obligation a homeowner has to inform prospective buyers of any and all defects in the home or on the property, such as environmental problems or code violations.

Equity

The amount of money the owner has invested in the property; the value of the property minus associated debts.

Encumbrance

A third party legal claim against the property.

Escrow

An arrangement whereby a third party holds funds for a buyer and seller until all terms of the agreement have been satisfied.

F-M

Floating interest rate

A variable interest rate usually tied to an index.

Foreclosure

The acquisition of real property by a lender from a mortgagor who has defaulted on the loan.

"Good faith" deposit (deposit in earnest)

An amount of money given to the seller along with an offer to purchase a home, usually subject to the home passing an inspection. The deposit is not a mortgage down payment, and the deposit is usually held by a third party until the contract is accepted by the seller.

Gross income

Total amount of income from all sources before taxes and operating expenses.

Housing-to-income ratio

A ratio used by lenders to determine whether an applicant is qualified for a mortgage. It equals total cost of housing divided by gross monthly income.

Lease-option

A method of financing in which a tenant has the option to buy a property after a specified period of time.

Listing

A list of properties for sale; listings can be restricted to specific housing markets, price ranges, or Realtors.

Market

A geographical area and/or specific category of potential buyers (or sellers).

M-R

Mortgage

Document pledging real property as collateral for the repayment of a loan. The lending institution is known as the "mortgagee" and the person borrowing money for a home is called the "mortgagor."

Mortgage insurance

Protects the lender against borrower's default on a loan. Also known as private mortgage insurance or PMI.

Multiple listing service (MLS)

A computerized database of all properties listed for sale.

Net worth

The amount of assets you have after subtracting all of your debts and liabilities.

Open house

Making your home available for inspection (often for a day or a weekend).

Points

A one-time fee charged by a lender for processing a mortgage loan. One point is equal to one percent of the amount of the loan.

Quitclaim deed

A document that transfers title and interest from seller to buyer without a warranty.

Realtor®

A member of the National Association of Realtors who represents buyers/sellers of homes in the purchase/sale of real property. A Realtor may include Realtor Associates, brokers, and/or agents.

R-W

Recording

Delivering real estate documents to a public official for inclusion in the public records.

Refinancing

Taking out a second loan to pay off the first, higher-rate loan.

Satisfaction

A document given to the borrower by the lender indicating that the debt has been paid in full.

Settlement statement

A full and detailed accounting of the sources and dispersion of all funds in a real estate transaction.

Title

The document that describes the ownership of real property.

Title company

A company whose business is to search the public records to determine the status or condition of the title to a parcel of real property.

Truth-in-Lending Act

A federal law requiring lending institutions to reveal all terms of a mortgage.

Underwriting

The process lenders undertake to determine whether a buyer will qualify for a mortgage loan.

Warranty deed

A document that guarantees the seller is transferring a clear title to the buyer.

Resources

••• Federal Programs •••

For loans, etc.

Federal National Mortgage Association (Fannie Mae)

Customer Education Group

3900 Wisconsin Ave. NW

Washington, DC 20016

For rural areas

Farmer's Home Administration (FmHA)

U.S. Department of Agriculture

14th and Independence St., SW

Washington, DC 20250

For discrimination, home improvement loans, etc.

U.S. Department of Housing and Urban Development (HUD)

451 7th St., SW

Washington, D.C. 20410

For information on state's housing agencies:

National Council of State Housing Agencies
444 North Capital St., NW
Washington, DC 20001

For 50¢ brochure "How to Buy a Manufactured Home":

FTC Office of Consumer and Business Education
Consumer Information Center
Department 427Y
Pueblo, CO 81009

For free "Your Rights as a Home Buyer" brochure:

Fair Housing Information Clearinghouse (FHIC)
PO Box 6091
Rockville, MD 20850
Mortgage Information
National Association of Mortgage Brokers
706 E. Bell Rd., Suite 101
Phoenix, AZ 85022

For free brochure "How to Shop for a Mortgage":

Mortgage Bankers Association of America
1125 15th St., N.W.,
Washington, D.C. 20005

••• Inspections & Environment•••

For finding out whether an inspector is certified:

National Institute of Building Inspectors (NIBI)

424 Vosseller Ave.

Bound Brook, NJ 08805

For names of inspectors doing business in your area:

American Society of Home Inspectors (ASHI)

1735 N. Lynn St., Suite 950

Arlington, VA 22209

For Radon Gas and Lead Paint information:

Environmental Protection Agency

Public Information Center

401 M St., S.W., PM-211B

Washington, DC 20460

••• Online Resources •••

◆ **Abele Owners' Network**

   http://www.owners.com

◆ **American Society of Home Inspectors**

   http://www.ashi.com

◆ **Back to the Farm**

   http://www.govbiz.com

◆ **Better Homes and Gardens Real Estate Service**

   http://www.bhglive.com/guidpags/res.html

◆ **Escrow Publishing Company**

   http://www.escrowhelp.com

◆ **Federal National Mortgage Association (Fannie Mae) Homestyle Program**

   http://www.fanniemae.com

◆ **Home Buyers Avenue**

   http://hba-1.com/index2.htm

◆ **Homebuyer's Fair**

   http://www.homefair.com/home

◆ **HomePath**

http://www.homepath.com

◆ **HomeScout**

http://www.homescout.com

◆ **HomeShark**

http://www.homeshark.com

◆ **Inman Real Estate News**

http://www.inman.com

◆ **Insiders' Guide Onlinesm-Relocation**

http://www.insiders.com/relocation/index.htm

◆ **International Home Information Network (IHIN)**

http://www.web1234.com/ihinfiles/default.html

◆ **Internet Real Estate Digest**

http://www.ired.com

◆ **Mortgage 101**

http://mortgage101.com

◆ **MSN Home Advisor**

http://homeadvisor.msn.com/ie

◆ **National Association of Home Inspectors (NAHI)**

http://www.nahi.org

◆ **National Association of Realtors**

http://www.realtor.com

◆ **Realty Locator**

http://www.realtylocator.com

◆ **Selling And Buying**

http://www.sellingandbuying.com

◆ **United States Department of Housing and Urban Development (HUD)**

http://www.hud.gov

◆ **Yahoo! Real Estate**

http://realestate.yahoo.com

••• Related Sites •••

◆ **Equifax, Inc.**

URL: http://www.equifax.com

◆ **Experian Information Solutions, Inc.**

URL: http://www.experian.com

◆ **Trans Union LLC**

URL: http://www.transunion.com

••• State Bar Associations •••

ALABAMA

Alabama State Bar
415 Dexter Avenue
Montgomery, AL 36104
mailing address:
PO Box 671
Montgomery, AL 36101
(334) 269-1515

http://www.alabar.org

ALASKA

Alaska Bar Association
510 L Street No. 602
Anchorage, AK 99501
mailing address:
PO Box 100279
Anchorage, AK 99510

http://www.alaskabar.org

ARIZONA

State Bar of Arizona
111 West Monroe
Phoenix, AZ 85003-1742
(602) 252-4804

http://www.azbar.org

ARKANSAS

Arkansas Bar Association
400 West Markham
Little Rock, AR 72201
(501) 375-4605

http://www.arkbar.org

CALIFORNIA

State Bar of California
555 Franklin Street
San Francisco, CA 94102
(415) 561-8200

http://www.calbar.org

Alameda County Bar
Association
http://www.acbanet.org

COLORADO

Colorado Bar Association
No. 950, 1900 Grant Street
Denver, CO 80203
(303) 860-1115

http://www.cobar.org

CONNECTICUT

Connecticut Bar Association
101 Corporate Place
Rocky Hill, CT 06067-1894
(203) 721-0025

http://www.ctbar.org

DELAWARE

Delaware State Bar Association
1225 King Street, 10th floor
Wilmington, DE 19801
(302) 658-5279
(302) 658-5278 (lawyer referral
service)

http://www.dsba.org

DISTRICT OF COLUMBIA

District of Columbia Bar
1250 H Street, NW, 6th Floor
Washington, DC 20005
(202) 737-4700

Bar Association of the District
of Columbia
1819 H Street, NW, 12th floor
Washington, DC 20006-3690
(202) 223-6600

http://www.badc.org

FLORIDA

The Florida Bar
The Florida Bar Center
650 Apalachee Parkway
Tallahassee, FL 32399-2300
(850) 561-5600

http://www.flabar.org

GEORGIA

State Bar of Georgia
800 The Hurt Building
50 Hurt Plaza
Atlanta, GA 30303
(404) 527-8700

http://www.gabar.org

HAWAII

Hawaii State Bar Association
1136 Union Mall
Penthouse 1
Honolulu, HI 96813
(808) 537-1868

http://www.hsba.org

IDAHO

Idaho State Bar
PO Box 895
Boise, ID 83701
(208) 334-4500

http://www2.state.id.us/isb

ILLINOIS

Illinois State Bar Association
424 South Second Street
Springfield, IL 62701
(217) 525-1760

http://www.illinoisbar.org

INDIANA

Indiana State Bar Association
230 East Ohio Street
Indianapolis, IN 46204
(317) 639-5465

http://www.ai.org/isba

IOWA

Iowa State Bar Association
521 East Locust
Des Moines, IA 50309
(515) 243-3179

http://www.iowabar.org

KANSAS

Kansas Bar Association
1200 Harrison Street
Topeka, KS 66612-1806
(913) 234-5696

http://www.ksbar.org

KENTUCKY

Kentucky Bar Association
514 West Main Street
Frankfort, KY 40601-1883
(502) 564-3795

http://www.kybar.org

LOUISIANA

Louisiana State Bar Association
601 St. Charles Avenue
New Orleans, LA 70130
(504) 566-1600

http://www.lsba.org

MAINE

Maine State Bar Association
124 State Street
PO Box 788
Augusta, ME 04330
(207) 622-7523

http://www.mainebar.org

MARYLAND

Maryland State Bar Association
520 West Fayette Street
Baltimore, MD 21201
(301) 685-7878

http://www.msba.org/msba

MASSACHUSETTS

Massachusetts Bar Association
20 West Street
Boston, MA 02111
(617) 542-3602
(617) 542-9103 (lawyer referral service)

http://www.massbar.org

MICHIGAN

State Bar of Michigan
306 Townsend Street
Lansing, MI 48933-2083
(517) 372-9030

http://www.michbar.org

MINNESOTA

Minnesota State Bar Association
514 Nicollet Mall
Minneapolis, MN 55402
(612) 333-1183

http://www.mnbar.org

MISSISSIPPI

The Mississippi Bar
643 No. State Street
Jackson, Mississippi 39202
(601) 948-4471

http://www.msbar.org

MISSOURI

The Missouri Bar
P.O. Box 119, 326 Monroe
Jefferson City, Missouri 65102
(314) 635-4128

http://www.mobar.org

MONTANA

State Bar of Montana
46 North Main
PO Box 577
Helena, MT 59624
(406) 442-7660

http://www.montanabar.org

NEBRASKA

Nebraska State Bar Association
635 South 14th Street, 2nd floor
Lincoln, NE 68508
(402) 475-7091

http://www.nebar.com

NEVADA

State Bar of Nevada
201 Las Vegas Blvd.
Las Vegas, NV 89101
(702) 382-2200

http://www.nvbar.org

NEW HAMPSHIRE

New Hampshire Bar
Association
112 Pleasant Street
Concord, NH 03301
(603) 224-6942

http://www.nhbar.org

NEW JERSEY

New Jersey State Bar
Association
One Constitution Square
New Brunswick, NJ 08901-1500
(908) 249-5000

NEW MEXICO

State Bar of New Mexico
5121 Masthead N.E
Albuquerque, NM 87125
mailing address:
PO Box 25883
Albuquerque, NM 87125
(505) 843-6132

http://www.nmbar.org

NEW YORK

New York State Bar Association
One Elk Street
Albany, NY 12207
(518) 463-3200

http://www.nysba.org

NORTH CAROLINA

North Carolina State Bar
208 Fayetteville Street Mall
Raleigh, NC 27601
mailing address:
PO Box 25908
Raleigh, NC 27611
(919) 828-4620

North Carolina Bar Association
1312 Annapolis Drive
Raleigh, NC 27608
mailing address:
PO Box 3688
Raleigh, NC 27519-3688
(919) 677-0561

http://www.ncbar.org

NORTH DAKOTA

State Bar Association of North
Dakota
515 1/2 East Broadway, suite 101
Bismarck, ND 58501
mailing address:
PO Box 2136
Bismarck, ND 58502
(701) 255-1404

OHIO

Ohio State Bar Association
1700 Lake Shore Drive
Columbus, OH 43204
mailing address:
PO Box 16562
Columbus, OH 43216-6562
(614) 487-2050

http://www.ohiobar.org

OKLAHOMA

Oklahoma Bar Association
1901 North Lincoln
Oklahoma City, OK 73105
(405) 524-2365

http://www.okbar.org

OREGON

Oregon State Bar
5200 S.W. Meadows Road
PO Box 1689
Lake Oswego, OR 97035-0889
(503) 620-0222

http://www.osbar.org

PENNSYLVANIA

Pennsylvania Bar Association
100 South Street
PO Box 186
Harrisburg, PA 17108
(717) 238-6715

http://www.pabar.org

Pennsylvania Bar Institute

http://www.pbi.org

PUERTO RICO

Puerto Rico Bar Association
PO Box 1900
San Juan, Puerto Rico 00903
(787) 721-3358

RHODE ISLAND

Rhode Island Bar Association
115 Cedar Street
Providence, RI 02903
(401) 421-5740

http://www.ribar.org

SOUTH CAROLINA

South Carolina Bar
950 Taylor Street
PO Box 608
Columbia, SC 29202
(803) 799-6653

http://www.scbar.org

SOUTH DAKOTA

State Bar of South Dakota
222 East Capitol
Pierre, SD 57501
(605) 224-7554

http://www.sdbar.org

TENNESSEE

Tennessee Bar Assn
3622 West End Avenue
Nashville, TN 37205
(615) 383-7421

http://www.tba.org

TEXAS

State Bar of Texas
1414 Colorado
PO Box 12487
Austin, TX 78711
(512) 463-1463

*http://www.texasbar.com/
start.htm*

UTAH

Utah State Bar
645 South 200 East, Suite 310
Salt Lake City, UT 84111
(801) 531-9077

http://www.utahbar.org

VERMONT

Vermont Bar Association
PO Box 100
Montpelier, VT 05601
(802) 223-2020

http://www.vtbar.org

VIRGINIA

Virginia State Bar
707 East Main Street, suite 1500
Richmond, VA 23219-0501
(804) 775-0500

Virginia Bar Association
701 East Franklin St., Suite 1120
Richmond, VA 23219
(804) 644-0041
http://www.vbar.org

VIRGIN ISLANDS

Virgin Islands Bar Association
P.O. Box 4108
Christiansted, Virgin Islands
00822
(340) 778-7497

WASHINGTON

Washington State Bar
Association
500 Westin Street
2001 Sixth Avenue
Seattle, WA 98121-2599
(206) 727-8200
http://www.wsba.org

WEST VIRGINIA

West Virginia State Bar
2006 Kanawha Blvd. East
Charleston, WV 25311
(304) 558-2456
http://www.wvbar.org

West Virginia Bar Association
904 Security Building
100 Capitol Street
Charleston, WV 25301
(304) 342-1474

WISCONSIN

State Bar of Wisconsin
402 West Wilson Street
Madison, WI 53703
(608) 257-3838
*http://www.wisbar.org/
home.htm*

WYOMING

Wyoming State Bar
500 Randall Avenue
Cheyenne, WY 82001
PO Box 109
Cheyenne, WY 82003
(307) 632-9061
http://www.wyomingbar.org

How to save on attorney fees

How to save on attorney fees

Millions of Americans know they need legal protection, whether it's to get agreements in writing, protect themselves from lawsuits, or document business transactions. But too often these basic but important legal matters are neglected because of something else millions of Americans know: legal services are expensive.

They don't have to be. In response to the demand for affordable legal protection and services, there are now specialized clinics that process simple documents. Paralegals help people prepare legal claims on a freelance basis. People find they can handle their own legal affairs with do-it-yourself legal guides and kits. Indeed, this book is a part of this growing trend.

When are these alternatives to a lawyer appropriate? If you hire an attorney, how can you make sure you're getting good advice for a reasonable fee? Most importantly, do you know how to lower your legal expenses?

When there is no alternative

Make no mistake: serious legal matters require a lawyer. The tips in this book can help you reduce your legal fees, but there is no alternative to good professional legal services in certain circumstances:

- when you are charged with a felony, you are a repeat offender, or jail is possible

- when a substantial amount of money or property is at stake in a lawsuit

- when you are a party in an adversarial divorce or custody case

- when you are an alien facing deportation

- when you are the plaintiff in a personal injury suit that involves large sums of money

- when you're involved in very important transactions

Are you sure you want to take it to court?

Consider the following questions before you pursue legal action:

What are your financial resources?

Money buys experienced attorneys, and experience wins over first-year lawyers and public defenders. Even with a strong case, you may save money by not going to court. Yes, people win millions in court. But for every big winner there are ten plaintiffs who either lose or win so little that litigation wasn't worth their effort.

Do you have the time and energy for a trial?

Courts are overbooked, and by the time your case is heard your initial zeal may have grown cold. If you can, make a reasonable settlement out of court. On personal matters, like a divorce or custody case, consider the emotional toll on all parties. Any legal case will affect you in some way. You will need time away from work.

A newsworthy case may bring press coverage. Your loved ones, too, may face publicity. There is usually good reason to settle most cases quickly, quietly, and economically.

How can you settle disputes without litigation?

Consider *mediation*. In mediation, each party pays half the mediator's fee and, together, they attempt to work out a compromise informally. *Binding arbitration* is another alternative. For a small fee, a trained specialist serves as judge, hears both sides, and hands down a ruling that both parties have agreed to accept.

So you need an attorney

Having done your best to avoid litigation, if you still find yourself headed for court, you will need an attorney. To get the right attorney at a reasonable cost, be guided by these four questions:

What type of case is it?

You don't seek a foot doctor for a toothache. Find an attorney experienced in your type of legal problem. If you can get recommendations from clients who have recently won similar cases, do so.

Where will the trial be held?

You want a lawyer familiar with that court system and one who knows the court personnel and the local protocol—which can vary from one locality to another.

Should you hire a large or small firm?

Hiring a senior partner at a large and prestigious law firm sounds reassuring, but chances are the actual work will be handled by associates—at high rates. Small firms may give your case more attention but, with fewer resources, take longer to get the work done.

What can you afford?

Hire an attorney you can afford, of course, but know what a fee quote includes. High fees may reflect a firm's luxurious offices, high-paid staff and unmonitored expenses, while low estimates may mean "unexpected" costs later. Ask for a written estimate of all costs and anticipated expenses.

How to find a good lawyer

Whether you need an attorney quickly or you're simply open to future possibilities, here are seven nontraditional methods for finding your lawyer:

1) **Word of mouth**: Successful lawyers develop reputations. Your friends, business associates and other professionals are potential referral sources. But beware of hiring a friend. Keep the client-attorney relationship strictly business.

2) **Directories**: The Yellow Pages and the Martin-Hubbell Lawyer Directory (in your local library) can help you locate a lawyer with the right education, background and expertise for your case.

3) **Databases**: A paralegal should be able to run a quick computer search of local attorneys for you using the Westlaw or Lexis database.

4) **State bar associations**: Bar associations are listed in phone books. Along with lawyer referrals, your bar association can direct you to low-cost legal clinics or specialists in your area.

5) **Law schools**: Did you know that a legal clinic run by a law school gives law students hands-on experience? This may fit your legal needs. A third-year law student loaded with enthusiasm and a little experience might fill the bill quite inexpensively—or even for free.

6) **Advertisements**: Ads are a lawyer's business card. If a "TV attorney" seems to have a good track record with your kind of case, why not call? Just don't be swayed by the glamour of a high-profile attorney.

7) **Your own ad**: A small ad describing the qualifications and legal expertise you're seeking, placed in a local bar association journal, may get you just the lead you need.

How to hire and work with your attorney

No matter how you hear about an attorney, you must interview him or her in person. Call the office during business hours and ask to speak to the attorney directly. Then explain your case briefly and mention how you obtained the attorney's name. If the attorney sounds interested and knowledgeable, arrange for a visit.

The ten-point visit

1) Note the address. This is a good indication of the rates to expect.

2) Note the condition of the offices. File-laden desks and poorly maintained work space may indicate a poorly run firm.

3) Look for up-to-date computer equipment and an adequate complement of support personnel.

4) Note the appearance of the attorney. How will he or she impress a judge or jury?

5) Is the attorney attentive? Does the attorney take notes, ask questions, follow up on points you've mentioned?

6) Ask what schools he or she has graduated from, and feel free to check credentials with the state bar association.

7) Does the attorney have a good track record with your type of case?

8) Does he or she explain legal terms to you in plain English?

9) Are the firm's costs reasonable?

10) Will the attorney provide references?

Hiring the attorney

Having chosen your attorney, make sure all the terms are agreeable. Send letters to any other attorneys you have interviewed, thanking them for their time and interest in your case and explaining that you have retained another attorney's services.

Request a letter from your new attorney outlining your retainer agreement. The letter should list all fees you will be responsible for as well as the billing arrangement. Did you arrange to pay in installments? This should be noted in your retainer agreement.

Controlling legal costs

Legal fees and expenses can get out of control easily, but the client who is willing to put in the effort can keep legal costs manageable. Work out a budget with your attorney. Create a timeline for your case. Estimate the costs involved in each step.

Legal fees can be straightforward. Some lawyers charge a fixed rate for a specific project. Others charge contingency fees (they collect a percentage of your recovery, usually 35-50 percent if you win and nothing if you lose). But most attorneys prefer to bill by the hour. Expenses can run the gamut, with one hourly charge for taking depositions and another for making copies.

Have your attorney give you a list of charges for services rendered and an itemized monthly bill. The bill should explain the service performed, who performed the work, when the service was provided, how long it took, and how the service benefits your case.

Ample opportunity abounds in legal billing for dishonesty and greed. There is also plenty of opportunity for knowledgeable clients to cut their bills significantly if they know what to look for. Asking the right questions and setting limits on fees is smart and can save you a bundle. Don't be afraid to question legal bills. It's your case and your money!

When the bill arrives

- **Retainer fees**: You should already have a written retainer agreement. Ideally, the retainer fee applies toward case costs, and your agreement puts that in writing. Protect yourself by escrowing the retainer fee until the case has been handled to your satisfaction.

- **Office visit charges**: Track your case and all documents, correspondence, and bills. Diary all dates, deadlines and questions you want to ask your attorney during your next office visit. This keeps expensive office visits focused and productive, with more accomplished in less time. If your attorney charges less for phone consultations than office visits, reserve visits for those tasks that must be done in person.

- **Phone bills**: This is where itemized bills are essential. Who made the call, who was spoken to, what was discussed, when was the call made, and how long did it last? Question any charges that seem unnecessary or excessive (over 60 minutes).

- **Administrative costs**: Your case may involve hundreds, if not thousands, of documents: motions, affidavits, depositions, interrogatories, bills, memoranda, and letters. Are they all necessary? Understand your attorney's case strategy before paying for an endless stream of costly documents.

- **Associate and paralegal fees**: Note in your retainer agreement which staff people will have access to your file. Then you'll have an informed and efficient staff working on your case, and you'll recognize their names on your bill. Of course, your attorney should handle the important part of your case, but less costly paralegals or associates may handle routine matters more economically. Note: Some firms expect their associates to meet a quota of billable hours, although the time spent is not always warranted. Review your bill. Does the time spent make sense for the document in question? Are several staff involved in matters that should be handled by one person? Don't be afraid to ask questions. And withhold payment until you have satisfactory answers.

- **Court stenographer fees**: Depositions and court hearings require costly transcripts and stenographers. This means added expenses. Keep an eye on these costs.

- **Copying charges**: Your retainer fee should limit the number of copies made of your complete file. This is in your legal interest, because multiple files mean multiple chances others may access your confidential information. It is also in your financial interest, because copying costs can be astronomical.

- **Fax costs**: As with the phone and copier, the fax can easily run up costs. Set a limit.

- **Postage charges**: Be aware of how much it costs to send a legal document overnight, or a registered letter. Offer to pick up or deliver expensive items when it makes sense.

- **Filing fees**: Make it clear to your attorney that you want to minimize the number of court filings in your case. Watch your bill and question any filing that seems unnecessary.

- **Document production fee**: Turning over documents to your opponent is mandatory and expensive. If you're faced with reproducing boxes of documents, consider having the job done by a commercial firm rather than your attorney's office.

- **Research and investigations**: Pay only for photographs that can be used in court. Can you hire a photographer at a lower rate than what your attorney charges? Reserve that right in your retainer agreement. Database research can also be extensive and expensive; if your attorney uses Westlaw or Nexis, set limits on the research you will pay for.

- **Expert witnesses**: Question your attorney if you are expected to pay for more than a reasonable number of expert witnesses. Limit the number to what is essential to your case.

- **Technology costs**: Avoid videos, tape recordings, and graphics if you can use old-fashioned diagrams to illustrate your case.

- **Travel expenses**: Travel expenses for those connected to your case can be quite costly unless you set a maximum budget. Check all travel-related items on your bill, and make sure they are appropriate. Always question why the travel is necessary before you agree to pay for it.

- **Appeals costs**: Losing a case often means an appeal, but weigh the costs involved before you make that decision. If money is at stake, do a cost-benefit analysis to see if an appeal is financially justified.

- **Monetary damages**: Your attorney should be able to help you estimate the total damages you will have to pay if you lose a civil case. Always consider settling out of court rather than proceeding to trial when the trial costs will be high.

- **Surprise costs**: Surprise costs are so routine they're predictable. The judge may impose unexpected court orders on one or both sides, or the opposition will file an unexpected motion that increases your legal costs. Budget a few thousand dollars over what you estimate your case will cost. It usually is needed.

- **Padded expenses**: Assume your costs and expenses are legitimate. But some firms do inflate expenses—office supplies, database searches, copying, postage, phone bills—to bolster their bottom line. Request copies of bills your law firm receives from support services. If you are not the only client represented on a bill, determine those charges related to your case.

Keeping it legal without a lawyer

The best way to save legal costs is to avoid legal problems. There are hundreds of ways to decrease your chances of lawsuits and other nasty legal encounters. Most simply involve a little common sense. You can also use your own initiative to find and use the variety of self-help legal aid available to consumers.

11 situations in which you may not need a lawyer

1) **No-fault divorce**: Married couples with no children, minimal property, and no demands for alimony can take advantage of divorce mediation services. A lawyer should review your divorce agreement before you sign it, but you will have saved a fortune in attorney fees. A marital or family counselor may save a seemingly doomed marriage, or help both parties move beyond anger to a calm settlement. Either way, counseling can save you money.

2) **Wills**: Do-it-yourself wills and living trusts are ideal for people with estates of less than $600,000. Even if an attorney reviews your final documents, a will kit allows you to read the documents, ponder your bequests, fill out sample forms, and discuss your wishes with your family at your leisure, without a lawyer's meter running.

3) **Incorporating**: Incorporating a small business can be done by any business owner. Your state government office provides the forms and instructions necessary. A visit to your state office will probably be

necessary to perform a business name check. A fee of $100-$200 is usually charged for processing your Articles of Incorporation. The rest is paperwork: filling out forms correctly; holding regular, official meetings; and maintaining accurate records.

4) **Routine business transactions**: Copyrights, for example, can be applied for by asking the U.S. Copyright Office for the appropriate forms and brochures. The same is true of the U.S. Patent and Trademark Office. If your business does a great deal of document preparation and research, hire a certified paralegal rather than paying an attorney's rates. Consider mediation or binding arbitration rather than going to court for a business dispute. Hire a human resources/benefits administrator to head off disputes concerning discrimination or other employee charges.

5) **Repairing bad credit**: When money matters get out of hand, attorneys and bankruptcy should not be your first solution. Contact a credit counseling organization that will help you work out manageable payment plans so that everyone wins. It can also help you learn to manage your money better. A good company to start with is the Consumer Credit Counseling Service, 1-800-388-2227.

6) **Small Claims Court**: For legal grievances amounting to a few thousand dollars in damages, represent yourself in Small Claims Court. There is a small filing fee, forms to fill out, and several court visits necessary. If you can collect evidence, state your case in a clear and logical presentation, and come across as neat, respectful and sincere, you can succeed in Small Claims Court.

7) **Traffic Court**: Like Small Claims Court, Traffic Court may show more compassion to a defendant appearing without an attorney. If you are ticketed for a minor offense and want to take it to court, you will be asked to plead guilty or not guilty. If you plead guilty, you can ask for leniency in sentencing by presenting mitigating circumstances. Bring any witnesses who can support your story, and remember that presentation (some would call it acting ability) is as important as fact.

8) **Residential zoning petition**: If a homeowner wants to open a home business, build an addition, or make other changes that may affect his or her neighborhood, town approval is required. But you don't need a lawyer to fill out a zoning variance application, turn it in, and present your story at a public hearing. Getting local support before the hearing is the best way to assure a positive vote; contact as many neighbors as possible to reassure them that your plans won't adversely affect them or the neighborhood.

9) **Government benefit applications**: Applying for veterans' or unemployment benefits may be daunting, but the process doesn't require legal help. Apply for either immediately upon becoming eligible. Note: If your former employer contests your application for unemployment benefits and you have to defend yourself at a hearing, you may want to consider hiring an attorney.

10) **Receiving government files**: The Freedom of Information Act gives every American the right to receive copies of government information about him or her. Write a letter to the appropriate state or federal agency, noting the precise information you want. List each document in a separate paragraph. Mention the Freedom of Information Act, and state that you will pay any expenses. Close with your signature and the address the documents should be sent to. An approved request may take six months to arrive. If it is refused on the grounds that the information is classified or violates another's privacy, send a letter of appeal explaining why the released information would not endanger anyone. Enlist the support of your local state or federal representative, if possible, to smooth the approval process.

11) **Citizenship**: Arriving in the United States to work and become a citizen is a process tangled in bureaucratic red tape, but it requires more perseverance than legal assistance. Immigrants can learn how to obtain a "Green Card," under what circumstances they can work, and what the requirements of citizenship are by contacting the Immigration Services or reading a good self-help book.

Save more; it's E-Z

When it comes to saving attorneys' fees, E-Z Legal Forms is the consumer's best friend. America's largest publisher of self-help legal products offers legally valid forms for virtually every situation. E-Z Legal Kits and E-Z Legal Guides include all necessary forms with a simple-to-follow manual of instructions or a layman's book. E-Z Legal Books are a legal library of forms and documents for everyday business and personal needs. E-Z Legal Software provides those same forms on disk and CD for customized documents at the touch of the keyboard.

You can add to your legal savvy and your ability to protect yourself, your loved ones, your business and your property with a range of self-help legal titles available through E-Z Legal Forms. See the product descriptions and information at the back of this guide.

Save On Legal Fees

with software and books from Made E-Z Products available at your nearest bookstore, or call 1-800-822-4566

EVERYDAY LAW MADE E-Z

Fast answers to 90% of your legal questions

Clear, reliable & up-to-date

Save costly legal fees & protect your rights

More than a reference... a complete do-it-yourself tool!

Stock No.: BK311
$29.95 8.5" x 11"
500 pages Soft cover
ISBN 1-56382-311-X

Everyday Law Made E-Z

The book that saves legal fees every time it's opened.

Here, in *Everyday Law Made E-Z*, are fast answers to 90% of the legal questions anyone is ever likely to ask, such as:

- How can I control my neighbor's pet?
- Can I change my name?
- What is a common law marriage?
- When should I incorporate my business?
- Is a child responsible for his bills?
- Who owns a husband's gifts to his wife?
- How do I become a naturalized citizen?
- Should I get my divorce in Nevada?
- Can I write my own will?
- Who is responsible when my son drives my car?
- How can my uncle get a Green Card?
- What are the rights of a non-smoker?
- Do I have to let the police search my car?
- What is sexual harassment?
- When is euthanasia legal?
- What repairs must my landlord make?
- What's the difference between fair criticism and slander?
- When can I get my deposit back?
- Can I sue the federal government?
- Am I responsible for a drunken guest's auto accident?
- Is a hotel liable if it does not honor a reservation?
- Does my car fit the lemon law?

Whether for personal or business use, this 500-page information-packed book helps the layman safeguard his property, avoid disputes, comply with legal obligations, and enforce his rights. Hundreds of cases illustrate thousands of points of law, each clearly and completely explained.

MADE E-Z™
PRODUCTS

Whatever you need to know, we've made it E-Z!

Informative text and forms you can fill out on-screen.* From personal to business, legal to leisure—we've made it E-Z!

PERSONAL & FAMILY

For all your family's needs, we have titles that will help keep you organized and guide you through most every aspect of your personal life.

BUSINESS

Whether you're starting from scratch with a home business or you just want to keep your corporate records in shape, we've got the programs for you.

  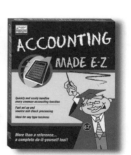

* Not all topics include forms   ss 1999.r2

E-Z to load, E-Z to run, E-Z to use!

**For our complete list of titles, call 1-800-822-4566
or visit our web site: www.MadeE-Z.com**

LEGAL

Easy to understand text explains how to fill out and file forms to perform all the legal tasks you need to—without all those legal fees!

TRAVEL & LEISURE

Learn health tips or travel all around the world, and then relax with a good crossword puzzle. When your work is done, we've got what you need!

MADE E-Z™
P R O D U C T S

Made E-Z Products, 384 S. Military Trail, Deerfield Beach, FL 33442
(800) 822-4566 • fax: (954) 480-8906
web site: http://www.MadeE-Z.com

ss 1999.r2

By the book...

MADE E-Z PRODUCTS™

MADE E-Z BOOKS provide all the forms you need to take care of business and save on legal fees – *only $29.95 each!*

Everyday Legal Forms & Agreements Made E-Z ISBN 1-56382-301-2
A do-it-yourself legal library of 301 ready-to-use perforated legal documents for virtually every personal or business need!

Corporate Record Keeping Made E-Z ISBN 1-56382-304-7
Keep your own corporate records current and in compliance... without a lawyer!

Managing Employees Made E-Z ISBN 1-56382-302-0
Over 240 documents to manage your employees more efficiently and legally!

Vital Record Keeping Made E-Z ISBN 1-56382-300-4
201 simple and ready-to-use forms to help you keep organized records for your family, your business and yourself!

Collecting Unpaid Bills Made E-Z ISBN 1-56382-309-8
Essential for anyone who extends credit and needs an efficient way to collect.

Available at:
Super Stores, Office Supply Stores, Drug Stores, Hardware Stores, Bookstores, and other fine retailers.

ss 1999.r2

★ E•Z Legal Kits	Item#	Qty.	Price Ea.‡
Bankruptcy	K100		$23.95
Incorporation	K101		$23.95
Divorce	K102		$29.95
Credit Repair	K103		$21.95
Living Trust	K105		$21.95
Living Will	K106		$23.95
Last Will & Testament	K107		$18.95
Buying/Selling Your Home	K111		$21.95
Employment Law	K112		$21.95
Collecting Child Support	K115		$21.95
Limited Liability Company	K116		$21.95
★ Made E•Z Software			
Accounting Made E-Z	SW1207		$29.95
Asset Protection Made E-Z	SW1157		$29.95
Bankruptcy Made E-Z	SW1154		$29.95
Best Career Oppportunities Made E-Z	SW1216		$29.95
Brain-Buster Crossword Puzzles	SW1223		$29.95
Brain-Buster Jigsaw Puzzles	SW1222		$29.95
Business Startups Made E-Z	SW1192		$29.95
Buying/Selling Your Home Made E-Z	SW1213		$29.95
Car Buying Made E-Z	SW1146		$29.95
Corporate Record Keeping Made E-Z	SW1159		$29.95
Credit Repair Made E-Z	SW1153		$29.95
Divorce Law Made E-Z	SW1182		$29.95
Everyday Law Made E-Z	SW1185		$29.95
Everyday Legal Forms & Agreements	SW1186		$29.95
Incorporation Made E-Z	SW1176		$29.95
Last Wills Made E-Z	SW1177		$29.95
Living Trusts Made E-Z	SW1178		$29.95
Offshore Investing Made E-Z	SW1218		$29.95
Owning a Franchise Made E-Z	SW1202		$29.95
Touring Florence, Italy Made E-Z	SW1220		$29.95
Touring London, England Made E-Z	SW1221		$29.95
Vital Record Keeping Made E-Z	SW1160		$29.95
Website Marketing Made E-Z	SW1203		$29.95
Your Profitable Home Business	SW1204		$29.95
★ Made E•Z Guides			
Bankruptcy Made E-Z	G200		$17.95
Incorporation Made E-Z	G201		$17.95
Divorce Law Made E-Z	G202		$17.95
Credit Repair Made E-Z	G203		$17.95
Living Trusts Made E-Z	G205		$17.95
Living Wills Made E-Z	G206		$17.95
Last Wills Made E-Z	G207		$17.95
Small Claims Court Made E-Z	G209		$17.95
Traffic Court Made E-Z	G210		$17.95
Buying/Selling Your Home Made E-Z	G211		$17.95
Employment Law Made E-Z	G212		$17.95
Collecting Child Support Made E-Z	G215		$17.95
Limited Liability Companies Made E-Z	G216		$17.95
Partnerships Made E-Z	G218		$17.95
Solving IRS Problems Made E-Z	G219		$17.95
Asset Protection Secrets Made E-Z	G220		$17.95
Immigration Made E-Z	G223		$17.95
Buying/Selling a Business Made E-Z	G223		$17.95
★ Made E•Z Books			
Managing Employees Made E-Z	BK308		$29.95
Corporate Record Keeping Made E-Z	BK310		$29.95
Vital Record Keeping Made E-Z	BK312		$29.95
Business Forms Made E-Z	BK313		$29.95
Collecting Unpaid Bills Made E-Z	BK309		$29.95
Everyday Law Made E-Z	BK311		$29.95
Everyday Legal Forms & Agreements	BK307		$29.95
★ Labor Posters			
Federal Labor Law Poster	LP001		$11.99
State Labor Law Poster (specify state)			$29.95
★ SHIPPING & HANDLING*			$
★ TOTAL OF ORDER**:			$

ss 1999.r2

See an item in this book you would like to order?

To order :
1. Photocopy this order form.
2. Use the photocopy to complete your order and mail to:

MADE E-Z PRODUCTS

384 S Military Trail, Deerfield Beach, FL 33442
phone: (954) 480-8933 • fax: (954) 480-8906
web site: http://www.e-zlegal.com/

‡*Prices current as of 10/99*

Shipping and Handling: **Add $3.50 for the first item, $1.50 for each additional item.**

Florida residents add 6% sales tax.

Total payment must accompany all orders.
Make checks payable to: Made E-Z Products, Inc.

NAME

COMPANY

ORGANIZATION

ADDRESS

CITY   STATE   ZIP

PHONE (   )

PAYMENT:

❑ CHECK ENCLOSED, PAYABLE TO MADE E-Z PRODUCTS, INC.

❑ PLEASE CHARGE MY ACCOUNT: ❑ MasterCard ❑ VISA   EXP. DATE

ACCOUNT NO.

Signature: _____
(required for credit card purchases)

-OR-

For faster service, order by phone:
(954) 480-8933

Or you can fax your order to us:
(954) 480-8906

CHECK OUT THE
MADE E·Z® LIBRARY

MADE E-Z GUIDES

Each comprehensive guide contains all the information you need to learn about one of dozens of topics, plus sample forms (if applicable).

Most guides also include an appendix of valuable resources, a handy glossary, and the valuable 14-page supplement "How to Save on Attorney Fees."

TITLES

Asset Protection Made E-Z
Shelter your property from financial disaster.

Bankruptcy Made E-Z
Take the confusion out of filing bankruptcy.

Buying/Selling a Business Made E-Z
Position your business and structure the deal for quick results.

Buying/Selling Your Home Made E-Z
Buy or sell your home for the right price right now!

Collecting Child Support Made E-Z
Ensure your kids the support they deserve.

Collecting Unpaid Bills Made E-Z
Get paid—and faster—every time.

Corporate Record Keeping Made E-Z
Minutes, resolutions, notices, and waivers for any corporation.

Credit Repair Made E-Z
All the tools to put you back on track.

Divorce Law Made E-Z
Learn to proceed on your own, without a lawyer.

Employment Law Made E-Z
A handy reference for employers and employees.

Everyday Law Made E-Z
Fast answers to 90% of your legal questions.

Everyday Legal Forms & Agreements Made E-Z
Personal and business protection for virtually any situation.

Incorporation Made E-Z
Information you need to get your company INC'ed.

Last Wills Made E-Z
Write a will the right way, the E-Z way.

Limited Liability Companies Made E-Z
Learn all about the hottest new business entity.

Living Trusts Made E-Z
Trust us to help you provide for your loved ones.

Living Wills Made E-Z
Take steps now to ensure Death with Dignity.

Managing Employees Made E-Z
Your own personnel director in a book.

Partnerships Made E-Z
Get your company started the right way.

Small Claims Court Made E-Z
Prepare for court...or explore other avenues.

Traffic Court Made E-Z
Learn your rights on the road and in court.

Solving IRS Problems Made E-Z
Settle with the IRS for pennies on the dollar.

Trademarks & Copyrights Made E-Z
How to obtain your own copyright or trademark.

Vital Record Keeping Made E-Z
Preserve vital records and important information.

KITS

Each kit includes a clear, concise instruction manual to help you understand your rights and obligations, plus all the information and sample forms you need.

For the busy do-it-yourselfer, it's quick, affordable, and it's E-Z.

ss 1999.r1

Index

L-R✦✦✦✦

S-Z✦✦✦✦